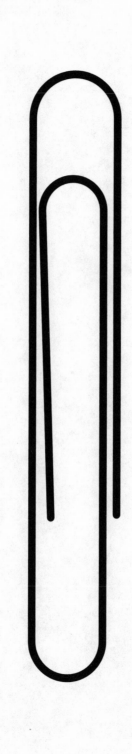

...WHAT NOW

...W

WHAT N

OW

MAKING SENSE OF **WHO YOU ARE**
AND **WHERE YOU'RE GOING**

*Marc Estes*

[RELEVANTBOOKS]

Published by RELEVANT Books
A division of RELEVANT Media Group, Inc.

www.relevantbooks.com
www.relevantmediagroup.com

© 2006 RELEVANT Media Group

Design by RELEVANT Solutions
Cover design by Ben Pieratt and Jeremy Kennedy
Interior design by Ben Pieratt and Jeremy Kennedy

Additional editing by City Christian Publishing.

For information or bulk orders:

RELEVANT MEDIA GROUP, INC.
100 SOUTH LAKE DESTINY DRIVE, SUITE 200
ORLANDO, FL 32810
407-660-1411

Library of Congress Control Number: 2005911207
International Standard Book Number: 0-9776167-5-4

06 07 08 09 10 8 7 6 5 4 3 2 1

Printed in the United States of America

Dedicated to the men whom God divinely placed in my path, who have guided me toward purpose and whose investment in me over the years could never be measured: Ellis Estes (the greatest father a man could ask for), Peter Friederici, Terry Edwards, Mike Shreve, Gary Beasley, and Frank Damazio. Each of your friendships and influences has led me to discover who I am and where I'm going. Thank you for everything.

# CON TENTS

# ACKNOW LEDGMENTS

The word *acknowledgment* seems to conjure up thin notions of appreciation or gratitude or other such niceties that often precede ribbon-cutting ceremonies and Academy Award speeches. In this case, the word *acknowledgment* isn't big enough. There isn't enough in it to describe the vast debt I owe a few key people. These few champions have been great blessings to me, both in my life and in this project.

### Pastor Frank Damazio

Over the past ten years, Pastor Frank has been a true pastor, mentor, and friend. I have garnered more from this man than perhaps any other person I know. He has shaped me, challenged me, encouraged me, and corrected me. He has believed in me and given me frequent opportunities when others may have doubted. His endless sacrifice and dedication to the local church and to his team have been an example that I can only hope to obtain someday. Pastor Frank, thanks for believing in me now and always.

### Casey Hill

Casey is one of my closest friends, as well as my executive assistant, though the title doesn't do this incredibly talented young man justice. I've rarely encountered the perfect blend of talent and character contained in this young man. Over the past several months, Casey has been instrumental in assisting me with gathering facts, chasing down interviews, and being my personal editor. Casey, you're a home run in my book.

### Gareth Gilpin

Gareth has been a very close friend and part of our pastoral team at City Bible Church. His ability to convey truth in a relevant way is second to none; he is a fine communicator and a wise man. Over the past two years, Gareth and I have worked hard to develop a massive volunteer effort in our local church through a ministry we call Connections. Our church is an infinitely better place to serve, due to the Connections ministry and Gareth's dedication.

### My Family

Listing your wife or family on an acknowledgment page may seem to underestimate the true cost and sacrifice they have given to a project like this. Many days off are spent in front of the computer, and many evenings are spent reviewing transcripts. I guess my saving grace on this project is that I've been able to include a few funny stories that have made us all laugh quite a bit. You'll just have to wait and see.

Sus, you are the most incredible wife a man could ever ask for. Your willingness to allow me the time to write and pursue this burden to write is greatly appreciated. Heather, Elisa, Aaron, and Kyle, thanks for being a great support and the best kids a dad could ask for. I am proud to see each of you pursuing your God-given dreams and living truly purposeful lives.

### Jesus

It may seem a little corny to pen a few personal words regarding my relationship with the Lord, but I must admit, He is the only reason I even take the time to write. If it weren't for Him, I would be nothing. Jesus, thank You for being with me through every word, thought, and expression. You truly are the Author; I am just the pen in Your hand. To You I give all the glory.

# FORE WORD

I remember when it happened for me. It was the "ah ha" moment that transformed my life and ministry. I was a homesick freshman at Florida State University, trying to adjust to the fast pace of college life without the security of my friends and family. My dorm was a veritable Mardi Gras atmosphere. It was the last place you'd expect to find the son of a preacher man.

In the middle of this confusing time, my relationship with Christ was in "coast mode." It's not like I was experimenting with drugs and dancing around with a lamp shade on my head, but I wasn't doing much good either. I guess you could say that my passion for Jesus was flaming out.

One night, as I knelt down in front of my rackety air conditioner, I started to pray. For the first time in quite a while, I didn't pray for my own needs. I found myself praying for a friend named Scott. Scott was the kind of guy that girls liked and men envied. He was good looking, athletic, and had a certain bad-boy edge. But he was empty inside. He had a terrible relationship with his parents and had been in the drug scene for years. Though his family had money, he had been arrested for burglary. He said it gave him an adrenaline rush.

On our way to class one day, Scott asked me a question that floored me. He said, "Something is different about you. You have something that I don't have. What is it?" It was the opportunity I had been praying for. Later that night, two amazing things happened. I led Scott in a prayer to begin his journey as a follower of Jesus Christ. And Christ led me into full-time ministry.

When I invited Scott to church with me that weekend, another life-altering experience clarified my life's direction. Seeing a church service through the eyes of Scott, I was embarrassed. The music was tired. The sermon was boring. The service was lifeless. Deep within, I felt this strong sense that I could do better. *If I ever go into church work,* I thought, *I will do whatever it takes to provide a biblically driven and creative experience that someone like Scott could understand.*

About twenty years have passed since those two events happened. I've lost some of my hair and memory, gained a few well-earned wrinkles, but my passion for the local church has only intensified. Quite simply, I love the local church. I love being a pastor. And I love hearing the stories of people like Scott who turn from darkness to light. God has been exceedingly gracious to me in allowing me to lead a church that reaches 20,000 each weekend in the Dallas-Fort Worth area. There is nothing like the excitement that comes from waking up every morning knowing you are doing exactly what you were made to do. And the journey that God takes you on is far more rewarding than anything you can imagine.

The book you're holding is a tool that I believe will help you discover that kind of excitement and fulfillment. Knowing that you are made in the image of God for a wonderful and strategic purpose in God's kingdom is incredible. Maybe you're waiting for an "ah ha" experience, and you just need a little help getting there.

Marc Estes does an amazing job of providing you with a book that will encourage you to discover your unique purpose in life. But he doesn't stop there. He provides you with practical assessment tools that will give you clarity and confidence. And he weaves it all together with stories of real people who have "been there and done that." My favorite element of the book is his repeated emphasis of finding your place in the body of Christ. Marc and I agree that serving others in the context of the local church is just about the best thing you can do for your spiritual growth. And it's the most exciting thing you can do this side of eternity.

I remember when it happened for me. I pray that Marc's book will be an integral step so it can happen for you too.

**Ed Young**
Senior Pastor, Fellowship Church, and Author of *The Creative Leader* and *You!*

# CONFESSIONS OF A SQUANDERED PAPER CLIP
## INTRODUCING LIFE ON PURPOSE

It seems that everyone would want to live life purposefully. That you picked up this book at all indicates you have at least some desire to make your life count for something greater than the sum of your efforts; that you're driven to achieve significance; that you are, on some level, compelled to become who you're supposed to be. There's an innate desire in all of us, who have been created in the image of God, to live a life bigger than ourselves.

Although this may be nearly everyone's intention, too often living a deliberate, purposeful life falls short of becoming a reality. For many, living life on purpose may have given way to "life just happens," as evidenced by broken dreams or deferred hopes. For a few, filling these blanks in their lives may have become a seemingly impossible, unreachable illusion. For others, the quest has been fueled with passionate dedication, but their lives end up being filled with entirely the wrong matter—unbridled energy is misapplied to voids that scream for real *substance*. Consumed with chasing worldly pursuits, they spend their lives building a reputation for themselves to impress people they don't like by obtaining things they don't need, only to end up as empty and confused as when they began. This is a book about avoiding that catastrophe altogether.

---

Lloyd's Bank of London undertook a study to find out what happens to a typical batch of paper clips as they are released throughout the workforce. Out of a batch of 100,000 paper clips, 3,916 were used to unplug tobacco pipes; 5,308 were used to clean under fingernails; 5,423 were used to pick teeth or scratch ears; 7,200 were used as hooks for belts, suspenders, or bras; 14,163 were snapped, broken, or otherwise twisted during phone conversations; 19,143 became mock card game chips; and approximately 25,000 became lost, swept up off the floor, or thrown away. Only 20,000 of the original batch of paper clips were actually used to clip papers together.[1]

Interesting. Only a minority of these paper clips, each one created for a specific function, were ever used for their intended design! The overwhelming majority were used to fulfill some other alternative purpose. Such is the tragedy today with many who claim to follow Christ; attempts at fulfilling their intended purpose go awry. This is neither God's will nor His desire.

---

God's intent is that we grab hold of our purpose and live life *deliberately*, not randomly. In Jesus' parable of the talents (Matt. 25:14–30), it becomes quite clear that each of us has been given a measure of gifts, talents, and abilities to invest during our lifetime. How we use or misuse them creates consequences. Ultimately, each of us will be held responsible for what we were given and whether we were faithful in making our lives count. This parable further illustrates that every person has been given opportunities to make a difference. Therein lie the challenge of your life and the intent of this book: live a deliberate, purposeful life!

**THERE'S AN INNATE DESIRE IN ALL OF US, WHO HAVE BEEN CREATED IN THE IMAGE OF GOD, TO LIVE A LIFE BIGGER THAN OURSELVES.**

As I write this, I must admit that I am on this life journey myself. I have not arrived at the final destination or mastered this pursuit. I face this challenge every morning when I wake and assess my efforts every evening when my head hits my pillow. On the flip side, God has revealed certain truths that have been very beneficial to my life and to those in the church where I am privileged to serve. It is within this context that I share these thoughts with the hope that you, the reader, will be stirred to live life with more purpose than ever before.

This book is divided into four parts. Part One has been written to assist you in understanding how unique you are and to point out that there is a very definite plan for your life. You are no accident! You were created with a purpose and plan.

Part Two is an in-depth look at how God made you, along with some very practical self-discovery tools. You'll find that no two persons will score exactly the same, which further validates your uniqueness and identity in Christ. You will see yourself—perhaps for the very first time—in the way God designed you to fill in the blanks of your life.

Part Three provides an implementation strategy, giving you specific direction on how you might fulfill your intended design by serving in the local church and being intricately involved as an important part of the body of Christ.

Part Four provides an opportunity for you to learn more about yourself, your purpose, and your opportunity to live life on purpose. I strongly urge you to take part in these exercises and discover what God already knows: that you have been singled out from all of humanity to accomplish something big. Let me challenge you not to approach this book as an "easy read." Take time to read each chapter, digest the Scriptures, and pray specifically through each point. Use the self-discovery tools and challenge yourself to make any changes necessary to provoke yourself to another level of usefulness and fruitfulness. If you're up to the challenge, let's begin the journey!

# PART ONE

## WHY HERE, WHY NOW?

# PART ONE

## WHY HERE, WHY NOW?

# CHAPTER ONE

# ON A JOURNEY ...
# GOING SOMEWHERE
## THE LIFE WITHOUT PURPOSE

"If people can't see what God is doing, they
stumble all over themselves; but when they attend
to what he reveals, they are most blessed."

—Proverbs 29:18, MSG

T hirteen-year-old Larry Walters first saw them when he walked into
a local Army-Navy surplus store. As magnificent as they were, most
would look at them and see ordinary weather balloons hanging from a ceiling.
Larry saw something more. Spellbound, the boy marveled that someday,
somehow, these balloons could carry him in the air! This idea became an
obsession that would capture his imagination for the next twenty years.

Then finally, on July 2, 1982, his big day arrived. Driven by years of planning
and dreaming, grown-up Larry Walters embarked on his mission to ride the
wind, carried solely by a bough of standard-issue weather balloons. Together
with a small group of friends in the backyard of his girlfriend's house in San
Pedro, California, Larry tied forty-two helium-filled weather balloons to a
Sears lawn chair, the entire ramshackle ensemble anchored by two nylon teth-
ers tied to the bumper of his friend's car. He secured himself comfortably into
his "cockpit" and, carrying only a BB gun (to shoot out balloons for descent),
gave the thumbs-up to cut the first tether.

If things had gone according to plan, Larry's drift would have gently carried him on the wings of the wind across the Southern California desert and placed him on the foothills of the Rocky Mountains in a couple of days. And the stuff dreams are made of—helium and a lawn chair—would have secured Larry Walters a place in the halls of greatness for all time, where he would spend his days hobnobbing with the other equally accomplished go-getters of his generation.

To say things didn't quite go as planned would be a gross understatement.

Forty-two weather balloons pack an anti-gravitational force that would make an astronaut squirm. When Larry's ground crew cut the first tether, the second tether easily snapped, launching Larry into the sky at a velocity of more than 1,000 feet per minute. So fast was his ascent that Larry lost his glasses. And after managing to shoot out only a few balloons, he accidentally dropped his BB gun, setting him precariously adrift with no maneuverable options.

For several hours he drifted in the cold air, climbing to more than 16,000 feet above the Los Angeles and Long Beach airports. A TWA pilot spotted Larry and radioed the tower with the strange report that he had passed a guy in a lawn chair at 16,000 feet!

Eventually Larry landed in a Long Beach neighborhood. Although entangled in some power lines, he was uninjured. When asked by a *New York Times* reporter why he had attempted such a risky feat, he answered, "Since I was thirteen years old, I've dreamed of going up into the clear blue sky in a weather balloon ... by the grace of God, I fulfilled my dream."[1]

Was there more to Larry's dream? We may never know. A few years after his weather balloon stunt, Larry hiked to a remote spot in Angeles National Forest and tragically ended his life, shooting himself in the heart at the age of forty-four.[2] Nobody knows exactly why; all we can speculate is that soaring to new heights in a lawn chair wasn't enough to fulfill Larry's yearning for purpose. Maybe he wasn't dreaming big enough. Maybe.

## The Journey to Somewhere Begins

What is your life dream? Why are you here? What triumph were you created to accomplish, or purpose to fulfill? Pause for a moment and think about it. Once you've identified your life mission and purpose, ask yourself what you are doing now to achieve it. How much time do you spend pursuing your ultimate reason for existence? How much of your resources are spent maximizing your life potential?

The truth is that we are all on a journey to somewhere, and it will end someday. It's how we live our lives that will determine our ending point—not only the *where*, but also the *why* and *for whom*.

For some, their destination is clear and their path is paved with unambiguous direction. For others, the path seems a little more

**IT'S HOW WE LIVE OUR LIVES THAT WILL DETERMINE OUR ENDING POINT— NOT ONLY THE WHERE, BUT ALSO THE WHY AND FOR WHOM.**

obscure and their journey only takes shape along the way, with detours and distractions at every turn. Perhaps the journey behind you was a nightmare and what you've found has disappointed you. Unfortunately, you can't wake up and start all over. Your journey is your life, and you have to accept where it takes you.

## Influences Along the Way

From the moment you are born, you are influenced by your parents. The culture you are born into will impact your worldview. The belief system you are taught will affect your morals and values. Your educational endeavors will shape your career path. Your friends will greatly influence your actions. Your eternal perspective will determine where you spend your time, energy, and finances. The power of influence will shape your thoughts and your actions. Your actions will create certain habits, which create a defined lifestyle. Your lifestyle shapes your destiny, ultimately defining your journey's end. Your concluded journey will clearly define whether your life had meaning and purpose.

If our journey in life is shaped by certain influences, it is important to understand these molding forces and decipher which ones we will allow to define our future.

## Influence of Culture

The culture you are immersed in shapes your life. Certain sectors of society have varying degrees of shaping power on your life. They include:

- Educational
- Entertainment
- Financial
- Media

- Political
- Religious
- Social
- Sports

You don't have to go very far to see how each of these areas has influenced your thoughts, taken some of your time, and even drained your wallet. In some cases they even have become more prominent than God Himself.

---

In 1966 John Lennon claimed that The Beatles were "bigger" than Jesus. In today's high-tech world, however, Jesus is, in fact, bigger. Consider the number of monthly searches for names, titles, and subjects through Google. Google processes more than 150 million searches a day and can now make relative comparisons among popular topics. According to figures released in April 2002, Jesus received an average of 850,000 searches every month, surpassing The Beatles' 830,000. Jesus wins!

But only momentarily. While Jesus received 850,000 searches, pop music icons Jennifer Lopez and Britney Spears received 1,135,000 and 2.5 million searches respectively.[3] It appears that pop culture's influence is shaping the minds of the masses.

---

## Influence of Relationships

At the core of humanity is a desire to be accepted and to belong. We long for significance. This hunger is woven deep into the fabric of our being and can only be fulfilled through a connection with those around us. However, these relationships can have both a positive and negative effect on our life goals and final destination.

The Bible states in 1 Corinthians 15:33, "Do not be misled: 'Bad company corrupts good character'" (TNIV). Proverbs 13:20 says it this way: "Walk with the wise and become wise" (TNIV). As a good friend once told me, "Be careful who you hang around, because you will become just like them." The rule applies to both good and bad relationships.

It would be idealistic to expect every relationship in your life to be without fault; some of your relationships are going to be less than desirable—that's just life. You may have dysfunctional parents or an abusive spouse. You may have to endure an irrational boss or kowtow to the needs of a "problem client." Regardless of whether these relationships were of your choosing or thrust upon you, they can have a significant influence on your life.

**Influence of Our Own Flesh**

One of our most commanding yet least restrained influences is our own flesh. Whether we like it or not, we were born with a relentless sinful nature that will pester us until we reach the grave. No matter how much we pray or fast, the sinful nature seems to rear its ugly head in the most peculiar ways. Today's world and its abundance of temptations don't make matters any easier. Keeping up with the Joneses has become an expectation for anyone with a desire to be somebody or get somewhere in life.

**OUR FLESH IS AN INTENSE AND COMPELLING FORCE, AND WE WOULD SERVE OURSELVES WELL TO ACKNOWLEDGE ITS INFLUENCE ON OUR LIVES AND MAKE EVERY ATTEMPT TO MINIMIZE ITS IMPACT.**

Jesus urged, "Do not store up for yourselves treasures on earth, where moth and rust destroy, and where thieves break in and steal. But store up for yourselves treasures in heaven, where moth and rust do not destroy, and where thieves do not break in and steal. For where your treasure is, there your heart will be also" (Matt. 6:19–21, TNIV).

The apostle Paul echoed the same challenge: "Therefore, I urge you, brothers and sisters, in view of God's mercy, to offer your bodies as a living sacrifice, holy and pleasing to God—this is true worship. Do not conform to the pattern of this world, but be transformed by the renewing of your mind. Then you will be able to test and approve what God's will is—his good, pleasing and perfect will" (Rom. 12:1–2, TNIV).

I battle this every day. Every morning I imagine myself having to unscrew my head from my shoulders, shake out all of the wrong thoughts and worldly pursuits, and fill it with God's thoughts and desires before reattaching it back onto my shoulders just to make it through another day. If you were totally honest with yourself, you would probably fall into the same category. Our flesh is an intense and compelling force, and we would serve ourselves well to acknowledge its influence on our lives and make every attempt to minimize its impact.

## Influence of the Enemy

Most people have the best intentions of living a purposeful life but are derailed somewhere down the road by what could only be identified as a negative spiritual influence.

Your soul's enemy is bent on distracting you from ever amounting to anything. He works overtime, enticing you to build for yourself a kingdom of material wealth, rather than a legacy of purpose. He develops strategies that entice you to pursue distorted means of fulfillment through careers, hobbies, and even relationships. He devises ways to lure you to the pleasures of this world for self-gratification. In the end, life becomes merely what happens to people between the cradle and the grave, rather than a resource they determine to make life count for eternity.

Jesus warned of the enemy's plan. "The thief comes only to steal and kill and destroy; I have come that they may have life, and have it to the full" (John 10:10, TNIV).

Jesus' intent is that you live an abundant life to the fullest extent, experiencing greatness, overcoming obstacles, and conquering sin. He aspires that you live every day impacting the world around you. He wants you to experience value and purpose in everything you do. He wants you to make life count, really count, for something greater than you ever imagined.

## Influence of God and His Kingdom

There is no greater influence in an individual's life than God. It is in Him that we have everything we need to live life. His Word tells us how we should think and act. His Spirit guides us, encourages us, and even assists us to see life through an eternal filter. And church guides us toward spiritual health, growth, and maturity. It is God and His kingdom that should be the shaping influence in our lives. Unfortunately, few allow this to happen.

If there were ever a person who understood the power of influence, it would be King David. At the end of his life, he shared some very personal yet profound thoughts with his son Solomon: "Acknowledge the God of your father, and serve him with wholehearted devotion and with a willing mind, for the Lord searches every heart and understands every desire and every thought. If you seek him, he will be found by you; but if you forsake him, he will reject you forever" (1 Chron. 28:9, TNIV).

**IT WOULD BE AN OMINOUS MISTAKE FOR US TO UNDERESTIMATE THE WEIGHT AND INFLUENCE OF GOD AND HIS KINGDOM IN OUR LIVES.**

David knew there were times when he allowed other influences to affect his destiny, and the last thing he wanted was for his son to make the same mistake. The same holds true for our generation; it would be an ominous mistake for us to underestimate the weight and influence of God and His kingdom in our lives.

## Measuring Your Personal Journey

Think about how your influences have shaped your life. Only by honestly answering some tough questions can you discover the real influences at work in your life:

- What's my purpose in life?
- What dreams do I have for my life?
- What am I doing now to reach my goal?
- What really excites me?
- Where do I spend my time?
- Where do I spend my money? What do I like to give to?
- Am I really living life on purpose, or merely letting life happen to me?

I don't know about you, but questions like these cause me to lose myself in self-reflection. I *want* to live on purpose, but do my actions line up with my intentions? If I am totally honest with myself, I have to admit there is need for improvement. It's not that I don't do things with purpose,

The average person who lives to be seventy spends twenty years sleeping, twenty years working, seven years playing, six years eating, five years dressing, three years waiting, more than two years smoking, more than two years in bed, two years doing miscellaneous things (which, incidentally, includes one year spent in church), one year on the telephone, and five months tying shoes.[4]

but do I do enough? Are there things that I enjoy doing that eat up time and energy needed to fulfill my purpose? Have I set certain financial goals that may appear to be overly aggressive and therefore cause me to devote more time toward securing my future here on earth, instead of in heaven?

It is wise to invest your money in preparation for the later years in life. We should be encouraged to enjoy life and prosper. But do we sometimes forget about kingdom purposes in the process? Could there be a lack of balance?

Thank God there are answers to all of life's quandaries, and they are found in one place only: the infallible Word of God. There, God has made it clear that we can become who we're supposed to be only by building our lives on proven biblical standards and by being wary of the devil's schemes.

God's will is for you to succeed. You are unique and special; there has never been, nor will there ever be, anyone else like you! He has chosen you for a greater purpose than you ever imagined—a journey, the end of which only you can discover. What you find at the end will be a beautiful legacy if you make the journey count.

# CHAPTER TWO

# LUCKY YOU
## HE CHOSE YOU ... GET USED TO IT

> "God, your God, chose you out of all the people
> on Earth for himself as a cherished,
> personal treasure."
>
> —Deuteronomy 7:6, MSG

K evin Conner's parents gave him up for adoption when he was three, setting him adrift in the foster care system of Australia for the first ten years of his life. The unstable environment was a tough place where he faced rejection, loneliness, and loss that come with being carelessly and helplessly abandoned. Kevin resigned himself to desolation.

When he was eleven, Kevin was transferred to a Salvation Army boarding institution, where he was introduced to Jesus Christ. "It was actually the first glimpse of hope I had ever experienced in my life," he says. But even though he had a genuine encounter with God, Kevin still struggled with thoughts of ending his young life.

"I climbed up a tree one day at age fifteen, considering how to hang myself," Kevin says. "I didn't want to be born, and I didn't ask to be born. But I remember trying to talk myself out of that tree. I thought to myself, *This is stupid!* I believed in God, and I was crying out to Him." So Kevin climbed back down, ready to give life another chance.

Kevin was twenty-four when he finally came to accept and understand the fact that God had chosen him for *something*. Though his circumstances certainly painted a picture quite opposite of his newfound revelation, something deep in his heart told him it was true. "I made an eternal decision that day to give myself completely to the Lord," he says.

From that commitment forward, Kevin has never turned back. "I found myself consumed by the Word of God. Every moment I could find would be spent absorbing anything that had to do with the Bible. I just needed to know more about God and His plan for me, as well as His plan for all of humanity." This insatiable hunger for God's Word during these years strengthened Kevin's commitment to serve God and His purposes.

Waverly Christian Centre, the church Kevin planted in Melbourne, Australia, (now pastored by his son Mark) now exceeds five thousand members. Kevin has written more than fifty books—expositions, doctrinal resources, and theological texts embraced around the globe by almost every denomination—which have left an indelible imprint on the Church.

It's a lesson in understanding that the promises of God far outreach any of life's obstacles. You could easily make the case that Kevin Conner is one of the greatest legacies of faith in our day.

But Kevin would be the first to correct you. "It's not what I have done that is important, but rather, 'Lord, what *else* can I do to serve You and Your people? As long as You give me another breath, there will always be something more I can do for You.'"[1]

## How Do You Feel About Yourself?

The concept of being individually created and chosen by God is a basic biblical concept. We learned it as children in Sunday school—"red and yellow, black and white, they are precious in His sight"—and we solidly believed it because, at that point, we hadn't learned the perceived "value" of being the same as everyone else. As children not yet influenced by commercialism or society, we accepted our uniqueness.

And then we grew up.

As adults, it's easy to take the devil's bait, comparing ourselves to what we see in popular culture, trying to become something *else* and therefore attaching value to an identity that was never meant to be ours in the first place. And when we learn that we can't adequately imitate that identity, our self-worth plunges and the things that stood in the way of achieving that identity become supposed faults to overcome. But God never intended for us to feel that way.

Embracing the fact that God, the Creator of the universe, had you mapped out on the drawing board before time began can be a hard pill to swallow in light of how we often view ourselves. Despite your faults (the perceived ones and the real ones), the idea that God chose you and created you for His purpose may be beyond your human comprehension, but it's entirely true!

How do you really feel about yourself? How do you think God feels about you? At your core, do you really believe that God cares for you? Do you really embrace the fact that you are important to Him and His purpose?

I think back to the dreadful moment every day in elementary school when Mrs. Logue would dismiss us for recess. You'd think getting out in the bright California sunshine would beat stay- ing inside learn- ing multiplication tables. But for this seven-year-old, the thought of lining

**REAL LIFE HAS A WAY OF THROWING US A RAPID-FIRE ONSLAUGHT OF CHALLENGES ALMOST EVERY DAY, VIGOROUSLY BACKING US INTO A CORNER.**

up against the wall once more to be chosen for dodgeball teams would make the breakfast milk in my stomach curdle.

My classmates Tommy and Brad loved the thought of lining up, and it's easy to see why: dodgeball is great when you're always chosen first! But for Lenny and me, lining up on that wall was humiliating. To add insult to injury, we ritualistically found ourselves the first easy targets for elimination. Huddled together in the back corner of the dodgeball square as the other team pummeled us, we were always the first ones out, dejectedly sent back to the wall to watch the more talented dodgeball enthusiasts enjoy the rest of the game. I would have opted for indoor multiplication any day.

Though the torment from those dodgeball days is over, I've come to learn that most of us have experienced similar frustrations in the game of life. Real life has a way of throwing us a rapid-fire onslaught of challenges almost every day, vigorously backing us into a corner. These unpredictable and unwelcome life experiences whittle away our confidence, reshaping us to think less of ourselves. We become deceived, thinking we are a cut under the rest and therefore insignificant to our peers, family, and, many times, the Guy up above. As a result, we are convinced that we'll never amount to much.

Fortunately, I have developed a completely different view of myself through the eyes of my heavenly Father. God's Word, in partnership with the Holy Spirit, has reshaped my self-worth and my potential for greatness to reflect how God sees me—not the way I think others see me or the way I saw myself previously. I have learned the hard way that how I see and feel about myself have a vast impact on how far I'll go in life. Therefore, I choose to believe that I am one of God's chosen and that He created me specifically this way. He cares for me and thinks I am fantastically unique.

## He Is a Personal God

Most people believe in some concept of God. Yet how we define God is as important as our belief in Him. Four percent of Americans today believe they are gods themselves. Another seven percent believe that God is the total realization of personal, human potential.[2] If you happen to believe this, be prepared to accept the colossal ramifications of being bound by your own human limitations. On the other hand, if you believe that God is unchangeable (Heb. 13:8), unequaled (Isa. 40:13–25), infinite (1 Kings 8:27), all-powerful (Jer. 32:17), ever-present (Ps. 139:7–12), and all-knowing (1 John 3:20), there is a much better chance that you will reach your intended destiny with the assistance of an incredibly powerful God who is willing to lead you every step of the way.

It is also important to understand that He is a personal God. He loves you (1 John 4:8,16). He will always be truthful with you (Ps. 117:2). You can count on His mercy when you fall short (Lam. 3:22–23). He is fair in every circumstance (Ps. 89:14) and, thankfully, very patient (Exod. 34:6–7).

What a relief to know that there is a loving God who is on our side, coaching us and believing in us. He is for you, not against you. Understanding that God is a personal God and that He possesses these unchangeable attributes brings added confidence that you can really make your life amount to something eternally meaningful.

## He Personally Created and Chose You

My wife and I had the wonderful privilege of adopting two mentally challenged Spanish-Indian boys, Aaron and Kyle, when they were just infants. Their biological parents were both mentally handicapped, homeless, and heavily involved in alcohol and drugs.

Through our years of foster care, we had felt our role was to provide a loving, safe environment for children until their existing home was stabilized. We never even considered adopting them. Aaron and Kyle were different though. Despite the implications we knew would be involved in caring for children with severe mental handicaps, we were confident God was asking us to *choose* these little boys, to pull them out of the state system and invest them into our home and family forever.

**GOD NOT ONLY CHOSE YOU, HE WANTS YOU TO COMPREHEND HOW IMPORTANT YOU ARE TO HIM.**

We have never regretted making that choice. Aaron and Kyle are both teenagers now and have become our very own—loved, accepted, and significant to our family. We belong together.

It's interesting to see how life teaches you some of God's most important secrets. I have come to realize that God didn't place me in Aaron and Kyle's path (although there may be some merit to this), but that He placed them in my path. Over the years, I have learned much more about the heart of God from my boys than they may ever learn from me. God has shown me, time and time again, that in the same way they were chosen, given a new chance at life, loved, and made part of our family, so I have been chosen and placed into the wonderful family of God, where I am greatly loved and accepted.

You too have been personally created and chosen by God Himself. He lovingly created you and placed you in your mother's womb, every strand of your DNA expressly designed by Him for your unique purpose. The psalmist wrote, "You know me inside and out, you know every bone in my body; you know exactly how I was made, bit by bit, how I was sculpted from nothing into something" (Ps. 139:15, MSG). You are no accident, but a deliberate act of creation, chosen to be part of God's divine plan. Through relationship with His Son, Jesus Christ, God has set you apart and called you by His grace. He has adopted you into His family … where you belong.

The primary cellist for the Los Angeles Philharmonic Orchestra accidentally left a 320-year-old Stradivarius cello outside his home one spring afternoon in 2004. Nearby video surveillance cameras revealed that a bicyclist pilfered the legendary instrument.

At the time it was stolen, the General Kyd—the cello named for the man who brought the instrument to England at the end of the eighteenth century—was valued at nearly $3.5 million, being one of only sixty cellos handcrafted by Antonio Stradivari in his Cremona, Italy, workshop.

About three weeks later, twenty-nine-year-old nurse Melanie Stevens found the instrument lying beside a dumpster about a mile from where it was originally stolen, still inside its silver-coated plastic case. A homeless man helped her load it into her car's trunk. Stevens asked her boyfriend, who was a cabinetmaker, to convert the old cello into a one-of-a-kind CD rack. "I had the idea to possibly put a hinge on the front," she said. "He would install little shelves inside, and it would be a very elaborate CD case."

Stevens didn't know the significance of the instrument until she saw a news report about it and contacted her attorney, who reported that the instrument was found. She was rewarded a handsome $50,000, which she donated to charity.

Robert Cauer, a Los Angeles-based instrument restoration specialist who had worked with the General Kyd for some twenty years, reported the valuable instrument was damaged but repairable and would be back in service by the following season. When asked about the prospect that the prized instrument could have been turned into the world's most expensive CD rack, Cauer said, "It's so abominable, I get sick when I hear it."[3]

## You Are Important to God

Being chosen by God is part of the Bible's love story. But it gets even better. God not only chose you, He wants you to comprehend how *important* you are to Him. Everything was created by God for God, but beyond that, we have a very special place in His heart above all of creation. "He brought us to life using the true Word, showing us off as the crown of all his creatures" (James

1:18, MSG). Unfortunately, many of us don't see the ornate value God has placed on us, and this limits our ability to really use this vital revelation as a primary tool for living life on purpose.

As an executive pastor of a sizable church, I see a fair share of people swept from their destiny as they discount their relationship with God. I get sick when I see it—priceless instruments handcrafted for greatness, ignoring their divine purpose. How foolish to neglect the call to greatness in order to fulfill any other purpose.

Read this Scripture out loud, inserting your own name:

"I, [*your name*], am chosen by God, chosen for the high calling of kingdom work, chosen to be a holy person, God's instrument to do His work and to speak out for Him, to tell others of the night-and-day difference He made in me–from nothing to something, from rejected to accepted."
–Adapted from 1 Peter 2:9-10.

We cannot place enough value on our importance in God's symphony. You and I will never know our true potential until we realize how much God loves us. Only when we understand that the Master Craftsman dotingly created us in His workshop before a single note had been written—that, while He gently sanded and polished us to a golden luster, He knew our considerable value; that it was only after He applied the bow and tuned our heart strings to perfect pitch that He would stamp His worthy name on us—will we appreciate the warm resonance of His call and surrender to His purpose.

# CHAPTER THREE

# SURPRISE! YOU'VE GOT A PURPOSE

## UNDERSTANDING THE CONCEPT THAT WILL CHANGE YOUR LIFE

> "I know what I'm doing. I have it all planned out—plans to take care of you, not abandon you, plans to give you the future you hope for. When you call on me, when you come and pray to me, I'll listen. When you come looking for me, you'll find me. Yes, when you get serious about finding me and want it more than anything else, I'll make sure you won't be disappointed."
>
> —Jeremiah 29:10–14, MSG

B ill's family fell apart when he was barely a teenager. His parents moved to Pinellas Park, Florida, where his father eventually left his mother. She went to work as a bartender, where she met a man who moved into the house and wasted no time becoming violently abusive toward her. Right about that time, Bill learned his father had died.

Bill began drifting away from home, sometimes for days at a time. He wandered the streets of Pinellas Park, bumming meals and becoming more cynical and hopeless with each passing day. Hungry, skinny, and struggling with rickets, Bill resigned himself to the odds invariably stacked against him.

One day Bill's mom led him to a concrete culvert built over a drainage ditch. She said, "I can't do this anymore … you wait here.'"

Bill remembers: "For three days I sat in the Florida sun on that concrete culvert. I didn't know where to turn. If I had known how to pray, I would have done it, but religion had no place in our home. All I could do was try to be brave and choke back the tears that would fill up my eyes. Mom never came back."[1]

As a young man trying to find his way through life alone, Bill found Jesus. In 1980, he moved to New York, where he discovered unexpected purpose: sharing the life-giving message of the Gospel with inner-city kids, illustrating the power of God to seek and save the lost with his own life.

Today, Bill Wilson is the senior pastor and founder of Metro Ministries in Brooklyn, reaching more than twenty thousand inner-city kids each week. His progressive mission is to find and rescue the children left behind in the battle-ground of drugs, violence, abuse, and filth. Metro Ministries provides a model for changing the lives of urban youth in hundreds of cities around the world.[2]

---

## Defining Purpose

Vine's Expository Dictionary defines *purpose* as "a deliberate intention." According to Dictionary.com, *purpose* is defined as "the object toward which one strives or for which something exists." These definitions masterfully describe God's purpose for your life. He expects you to make the quest for purpose your highest priority. God has a reason for everything He does. Therefore, His purposes for you are deliberate and unchangeable. Careful planning goes into all His works.

In his book *The Foundations of Christian Doctrine*, author Kevin Conner writes, "All of God's purposes proceed from His person. What He does is always consistent with who He is. The kind of person He is dictates the kind of things He does ... The only way man will be able to find fulfillment in life is to discover the reasons why he was created, and fulfill them ... Man should be endeavoring to discover and fulfill the reasons God had in mind for creating him."[3] In other words, discovering purpose means discovering what God created you to accomplish. Purpose is God-initiated and has a God-centered outcome. It isn't merely an adventurous pursuit to subsidize a human, egoistic need, and it definitely has eternal significance.

## God's Fourfold Purpose for Mankind

Imagine turning on a garden hose full blast and leaving it to whip around the yard on its own. All at once, everything and nothing gets wet. Such is the unbridled search for purpose outside the framework of God's influence on our lives. Left to our own impulses, we effect few results, if any. Without the life-changing influence of God, finding purpose is like a long drive out of town for the same cup of coffee you could find just around the corner.

J ohn Smith is a man on a mission. You may have heard of this thirty-two-year-old man—who now goes by "Winter"—whose quest is to visit every Starbucks establishment in the world. Working only enough to fund his ongoing caffeine crusade, Winter carefully plans each journey, meticulously mapping coordinates of each Starbucks location before taking to the road. He sleeps in his car, which has no air conditioning and smells like stale coffee, visiting as many as twenty-eight stores in a single day.

Winter's discontent with all things local has lasted seven years thus far, taking him to 4,122 stores in North America, 114 in Great Britain, and fifty-three in Japan. Though he is on track with his mission, his java journey won't end anytime soon; Starbucks opens an average of ten new stores around the world each week.[4]

I have one question for Winter: why? Here's a guy, apparently with loads of time on his hands and one wicked caffeine addiction (and likely a need for a strong breath mint), whose pursuit of purpose has taken him around the world to Starbucks more times than the average Christian has attended church. He's a living, breathing human curio, squandering everything—time, resources, energy—on accomplishing a futile mission. It just doesn't make sense, either practically or eternally.

Before we make any attempt to uncover our purpose—that one specific thing God created us to accomplish—we need to understand something very important: since the dawn of time, God has given mankind a fourfold purpose to achieve—relationship, character, function, and reproduction—that is at the foundation of everything else we do in life. Getting this right will set the precedent for our unique individual purposes and how well we finish the journey of life.

### Relationship
The very first reason God created man was to have relationship with him. God desires to have a personal, intimate, ongoing, vibrant, healthy relationship with you (see John 14:16–20, 23).

### Character
The second reason God created man was to impart His nature into him. God wants each of us to have His character and image. We were created in the likeness of God and should, therefore, desire to display His likeness and character as we fulfill our purpose (see Genesis 1:26; Romans 8:28–29; 2 Corinthians 3:18; Hebrews 1:3).

### Function
The third reason God created man was to appoint him as overseer of the earth and all its inhabitants. We are His ambassadors and are to rule over all that He has entrusted to us, both individually and globally (see Genesis 1:26, 28; Genesis 3; Luke 10:19).

### Reproduction
Finally, we were created to reproduce, both naturally and spiritually. God not only desires to see new children brought into the world that will be raised in the ways of God, He also wants each of us to take the message of Jesus Christ to those who are in desperate need of finding their reason for existence (see Genesis 1:28; John 15:16; Acts 6:7; Colossians 1:10).

Unfortunately, most people never fully understand God's fourfold purpose for mankind as He intended it. Relationship morphs into exploitation, character becomes deception, function gives way to delegation, and reproduction halts altogether. Consequently, the concept of purpose becomes a means to achieve status, to gain luxuries, and to retire early and overindulged. Responding to daily needs and circumstances becomes part of life's routine and habits. There may be variant forms of dreams to pursue, vague ideas of mountains to scale, but not real purpose. In essence, without

**GOD HAS SET US UP FOR SUCCESS; OUR ROLE IS TO RESPOND.**

God influencing you, your life has the significance and hope of a dead person. How sad for those who are far from Him … and yet how very true.

The enemy of your soul will always, without hesitance, try to send you the message that you're dead to the fourfold purpose of God, that your specific individual purpose has been inactivated, and that you might as well abandon pursuit of your dreams. If he can't convince you it's true, then he'll try to shake you up, freak you out, and cause emotional paralysis. Only the tenacious will power through the fog of deception and fight for the signs of life—relationship, character, function, and reproduction—that are actively propelling you to make your journey count.

There's an old saying that goes, "The bee is praised; the mosquito is swatted."[5] Think about it! It isn't so much how busy you are, but rather *why* you are busy.

William Marsten, a prominent psychologist, asked three thousand people, "What do you have to live for?" A full 94 percent responded that they had no definitive purpose for their lives. Sadly, Marsten's survey proves that so many people live what Thoreau called "lives of quiet desperation"—enduring, waiting, wondering what their lives are all about, hoping their purpose will suddenly become clear to them in a divinely inspired moment. Meanwhile, they simply survive, mechanically going through the motions of living without ever experiencing the spark of aliveness! They grow cold, begin to lose color, and slowly fade away. They watch their dreams slip through their fingers and become increasingly fearful that life will completely fizzle out before they experience any true joy or deep sense of purpose.[6] Had they not shirked their responsibility to relationship, character, function, and reproduction in the kingdom of God, their journey would have ended quite differently.

## Our Purpose Requires a Response

You knew there was a catch, didn't you? Up until this point you may have been thinking all this purpose stuff sounds too good to be true. "All I have to do is believe, and my life will be full of purpose and destiny." Well, that is only half true. Let's not forget that we have a significant part to play. God has set us up for success; our role is to respond.

The second part of Jeremiah 29:10–14 shifts the attention from God's promises to our responsibility. "When you call on me, when you come and pray to me, I'll listen. When you come looking for me, you'll find me. Yes, when you get serious about finding me and want it more than anything else, I'll make sure you won't be disappointed" (TNIV).

When *we* call and pray … *He* will listen. When *we* look to Him for direction, wisdom, understanding, and grace … *He* will be there. When *we* get serious about seeking Him to find

**HOW CAN YOU MAKE THE MAJOR DECISIONS OF LIFE UNLESS YOU FIRST CONSIDER YOUR PURPOSE?**

His purpose for our lives and when we want it more than our worldly enticements and hang-ups … *He* will blow our minds by revealing our purpose, and it will be more than anything we have ever dreamed of. In other words, our responsibility is our response to *His* ability. It's that easy.

Responding to His ability requires that you take initiative to seek Him. There are three key life-truths that will immediately help you in applying God's purpose to your life.

**Seek Him for the reason you exist.**
I am often approached by people asking for advice regarding important life decisions. One of my first replies is: "Tell me, what is your life purpose? Why do you think you were created?" This is often met with bewilderment. They simply asked a question and were looking for some logical, pastoral response. They definitely weren't prepared for a philosophical journey into God's deeper purpose for their life. But if you really stop to think about it, how can you make the major decisions of life unless you first consider your purpose?

**Seek Him to make life decisions that align with your purpose.**
Once you have a better understanding of your purpose, keep this revelation at the forefront of every decision you make. Make decisions that are driven by purpose and not emotions, impulses, or circumstances.

I look back at some of the major decisions I have made in my life, and I am satisfied with most of them. I remember my decision to leave my professional career and go into full-time ministry. I had been with a company for almost ten years. The owners had become like parents to me. They poured their lives into my family. Financially I was positioned very well, owning a small percentage in the company. In every aspect I was set!

The challenge was that God had another purpose for me that He had clearly revealed. I knew He would ask me to make a choice between my plans and His purposes. I really enjoyed my job and deeply loved my boss and his family. I knew that making a decision to leave, after all they had invested into me, could appear to be a slap in their face. But when the time came, I had to make the life decision that aligned with my purpose.

That decision was one of the most difficult in my life. Many people very close to me, including family members, didn't see the logic in leaving everything I had ever worked for. The fact that I would walk away from a solid career and step into ministry where there were no guarantees was ludicrous to the natural mind.

Tough decisions—regarding career changes, moving to a new city, and marriage—come for everyone. Unless these decisions are based solely on God's purpose for your life, you may find yourself second-guessing them when the road gets bumpy. However, if you approach them with the full confidence of knowing who you are and where you're going, you can be certain of them despite hardships.

**Seek Him to stay purpose-minded daily.**
Beyond the few major decisions you will make regarding your future, a vast spectrum of seemingly small decisions will bombard you every day.

- Should I get up and pray or snooze a few more minutes?
- Should I read my Bible or watch this television program?
- Should I leave church right away to avoid the traffic jam or stay and meet some new people?
- Should I buy that new boat or contribute to the church building fund?

Only you can make the right choice. Paul said, "Be very careful, then, how you live—not as unwise but as wise, making the most of every opportunity, because the days are evil. Therefore do not be foolish, but understand what the Lord's will is" (Eph. 5:15–17, TNIV).

Making daily choices based on purpose will require changing some habits and thought

Start your journey by defining the reason you exist. (Hopefully, the remaining chapters of this book will help you clarify and articulate your purpose.) In addition, pray about it. Read God's Word. Seek counsel from your pastor or someone you respect. Remember, if you ask God, He would love to tell you.

patterns. Every morning in my devotional time, I have made it a habit to ask the Lord to remind me of my purpose for that day. I ask Him to show me ways I can redeem the time. I dedicate myself afresh and ask for His support and His help to stay on track. I can't say that I have mastered it fully, but with much prayer and the help of the Holy Spirit, I have learned to press on toward the mark and make purpose-based decisions.

Purpose has feet. In other words, purpose requires the intentional decision to take one step, then another, and another. The challenge of finding purpose and aligning your life to it will require you to take action, seeking God's direction and responding to His ability along the journey of life.

Eugene Peterson does a masterful job translating Paul's comments regarding this subject. "I'm not saying that I have this all together, that I have it made. But I am well on my way, reaching out for Christ, who has so wondrously reached out for me. Friends, don't get me wrong: By no means do I count myself an expert in all of this, but I've got my eye on the goal, where God is beckoning us onward—to Jesus. I'm off and running, and I'm not turning back" (Phil. 3:12–14, MSG).

# CHAPTER FOUR

# UNFATHOMABLE YOU
## YOU'RE SPECIAL, YOU'RE UNIQUE

> "Oh yes, you shaped me first inside, then out; you
> formed me in my mother's womb. I thank you,
> High God—you're breathtaking! Body and soul,
> I am marvelously made! I worship in adoration—
> what a creation! You know me inside and out, you
> know every bone in my body; you know exactly
> how I was made, bit by bit, how I was sculpted
> from nothing into something. Like an open book,
> you watched me grow from conception to birth;
> all the stages of my life were spread out before
> you, the days of my life all prepared
> before I'd even lived one day."

—Psalm 139:13–16, MSG

O n June 25, 1950, without warning or declaration of war, North Korean forces crossed the dividing line at the thirty-eighth parallel and invaded South Korea, igniting the Korean War, pitting brother against brother, and dividing families. Soldiers from the Allied Forces—Australia, Belgium, Britain, France, the Netherlands, the United States, and others—descended on the shores of the Korean peninsula to defend the South, fighting a bloody war that would leave nearly four million Koreans dead, two-thirds of them civilians.

Perhaps the most aching tragedy stemming from the Korean War was the blight of more than 100,000 orphans left to wander the war-torn streets alone. One of these was a girl named Stephanie Fast.

From the age of four, a mere toddler on the conflict-ravaged streets of Korea, Stephanie learned to survive. She learned how to kill and eat field mice and locusts, gather grasses and roots, and find shelter in the mountain caves during the summertime. But in the winter, when Stephanie came down from the mountains to find food and shelter in the city, she realized she was different (having a Korean mother and an Allied soldier father).

"I lived with continual physical and mental abuse on the street," she says. "I believed they could do whatever they wanted to me because I wasn't a person. I was inhuman. I was dirty. I saw with my own eyes little ones younger than me die all the time, and it didn't faze me one bit. Death was common."

One day some men kidnapped her and another girl, took them to an abandoned building, and tortured them. The other girl was eventually eaten by rats. "I had tasted many kinds of bitterness and many kinds of abuse, but for the first time I knew what hate was. I hated those men with a passion ... I swore at the age of six that, no matter how they hurt me physically, they weren't going to get to me. I wasn't going to let anyone see me beg for mercy! There was no way they were going to touch my heart—or so I thought."

For a long time, she wondered why she had survived. "I was tied to a water wheel one time and continually dunked, and I hoped I would die. I was taken to a rice paddy another time and buried alive. Another time someone threw me into a well and left me there for three days. And in every one of those situations, I should have died."

What Stephanie didn't realize was that emotionally she was already dead.

When she was seven years old, a cholera epidemic swept through Korea, killing thousands of people, including street orphans. Stephanie contracted the disease and began to die.

About that time, on the heels of the Korean War, World Vision, an organization dedicated to helping children, began sending workers out into the streets to gather the youngest together into orphanages (there simply wasn't room for all of them, so they focused on the youngest ones). A Swedish nurse by the name of Iris Eriksson saw Stephanie lying in a heap of garbage and rubble, dying of cholera, when God quietly spoke to her heart: "That girl has a purpose. I want you to rescue her." Eriksson later reported that her initial response was, "But God, she's almost dead, and she's too old …" But the persistent voice of the Lord continued: "You take her home with you!" Eriksson relented. She took the girl and nursed her back to health.

Eventually, Iris Eriksson found a place for Stephanie: a World Vision orphanage where, as the oldest child, Stephanie's duties included having to wash the dirty diapers of all the infants who lived there.

"I liked being in that orphanage because, for the first time, I found something that I could love: I loved children. And these little ones were tiny and helpless and the workers were too busy to really love each one of them individually. But I remember spending hours holding little ones in my arms, loving them."

When Stephanie was nine, a foreign couple visited the orphanage with the intent to adopt a baby boy. Instead, they adopted Stephanie.

"I was nine years old, but I didn't even weigh thirty pounds. I had worms in my body, lice in my hair, boils on my skin, scars on my body; I was not a pretty little thing. He came up to me, rattled off something to me in English, and I looked up at him. He took that huge hand of his and laid it upon my face, and it seemed to cover my whole face and half of my body. And it felt so good. My mother was watching from across the courtyard, and my dad was standing in front of me. At the same moment, God spoke to both of them and said, 'That's the one for you.'"

Think about the odds. Stephanie should have been snuffed out as an infant. She should have been killed as a four-year-old on the streets. She should have been eaten by rats and died of starvation by the age of six. She should have succumbed to cholera at the age of seven. She should have been passed over by the nurse who rescued her. She should have been overlooked by the foreign couple. But the overwhelming, wonderful truth is that God had something special in mind for Stephanie.[1]

## God's Creation Is Special and Unique

As a child, I was fascinated by the planets and stars. My father was an aero-
nautic engineer and partly responsible for landing men on the moon. I can
remember getting a small telescope from my father for my birthday one year
and positioning it on the back deck of our home in Southern California.
I remember looking through my new telescope and discovering a whole
new dimension of creation I never knew existed. I saw millions of stars and
wondered, *Who put them there? Why do they twinkle like that? Why don't they
fall?* I remember sitting out one night, in my naivety, on a quest to count the
number of stars in the sky. Surely with a little time and effort I could count
them in a single evening, right?

It is estimated that there are as many as 200 billion galaxies in the observable
universe. We aren't able to see all of them yet, since we currently can't build
a telescope big enough to peek into the farther reaches of space. Scientists
believe the number of stars in the universe is about 50,000 billion billion.[2]
That's 50,000 followed by eighteen zeros!

Staggering statistics like these bring at least partially fathomable meaning to the
phrase "God is awesome." God called this vast universe into existence, and
He knows every star by name. The Bible says, "He determines the number
of the stars and calls them each by name. Great is our Lord and mighty in
power; his understanding has no limit" (Ps. 147:4–5, TNIV). That, my friend,
is a bunch of names. You think about coming up with 50,000 billion billion
names! I have four kids, and I can't even remember their names all the time.
But God knows each star individually. For God to intimately know each of
the six billion people on the planet is easy!

David tried to understand this same mathematical perspective. He wrote,
"When I consider your heavens, the work of your fingers, the moon and the
stars, which you have set in place, what are mere mortals that you are mindful
of them, human beings that you care for them? You have made them a little
lower than the heavenly beings and crowned them with glory and honor" (Ps.
8:3–5, TNIV).

Even beyond the splendor and expanse of a universe that we can't even
understand, God still looks at you as His greatest achievement. He created
50,000 billion billion stars, but none of them is as beautiful as you. You are
His masterpiece!

It has been calculated that since the beginning of man, more than fifteen to twenty billion people have been born. Some who believe that man has been around for millions of years (we're not going to debate that) estimate the number to be upward of ninety-six billion. In either case, that's a lot. Currently, there are more than six billion people alive today. And every person is completely different than any other human being.

Here's how: DNA molecules can unite in an infinite number of ways. The closest number we can figure is 10 to the 2,400,000,000th power. That number represents the likelihood that you'd ever find somebody just like you. If you were to write out that number, with each zero being one inch wide, you'd need a strip of paper 37,000 miles long. In fact, if the DNA strands from your body were stretched out in sequence, they would reach to the sun and back (93 million miles) four hundred times.

In a twenty-four hour period your heart will beat 103,689 times. Your blood will travel more than 168,000,000 miles through your veins. You will breathe 23,040 times. You will move more than 750 muscles, speak 4,800 words, and exercise more than seven billion brain cells.[3]

Your uniqueness is a scientific fact. When God made you, He broke the mold. There has never been, and will never again be, anyone just like you. Your uniqueness is unfathomable!

## You Are Special and Unique

Now that we have a somewhat clear understanding of the facts, let's try to comprehend the reason behind them. Beyond the perplexities of science is a much more important spiritual purpose—the purpose for your existence. We have already established in the previous two chapters that God chose you before there was time and that you have been given a specific purpose. The revelation of who God made you and what He intended you to do is what makes you special and unique. The Bible says, "Many, Lord my God, are the wonders you have done, the things you planned for us. None can compare with you; were I to speak and tell of your deeds, they would be too many to declare" (Ps. 40:5, TNIV).

You have been created in the image of God for the purposes of God. When He said, "Let us make man" (Gen. 1:26–31), He wanted to call attention to the formation of mankind as one of preeminent importance. Barnes Commentary expands this thought:

The divine blessing is now pronounced upon man. It differs from that of the lower animals chiefly in the element of supremacy. Power is presumed to belong to man's nature, according to the counsel of the Maker's will. It is therefore necessary that we should receive from high heaven a formal charter of right over the things that were made for man. He is therefore authorized, by the word of the Creator, to exercise his power in subduing the earth and ruling ... this is the meet sequel of his being created in the image of God.[4]

This passage is about you!

All of creation serves some form of purpose, but you were created to serve His *divine* purpose. That makes you special. In all of humanity and the history of time, He has uniquely made you to fit into one place with one purpose that no one else can fulfill.

**ALL OF CREATION SERVES SOME FORM OF PURPOSE, BUT YOU WERE CREATED TO SERVE HIS DIVINE PURPOSE.**

God didn't create anything by accident. He would never create something, place a purpose on it, and withhold the tools necessary to accomplish its objective.

We have each been outfitted for a specific purpose. Some lead, others administrate. Some love to teach while others love to share their faith. Some were born to create things while others are passionate about management. Paul said, "There are different kinds of gifts, but the same Spirit distributes them. There are different kinds of service, but the same Lord. There are different kinds of working, but in all of them and in everyone it is the same God at work" (1 Cor. 12:4–6, TNIV). Each of us has been uniquely made in order that we might successfully fulfill the purpose to which we were called. God's intended purpose for your life is substantiated by the way He created you.

## How God Made You

God has given you certain gifts, talents, and abilities. He has placed deep within your heart certain passions for people, issues, and areas of ministry. He has allowed experiences in life to shape your character, perspective, and worldview. He has also given you the opportunity to grow and mature in Christ, in hopes that you might maximize the time you have been given for

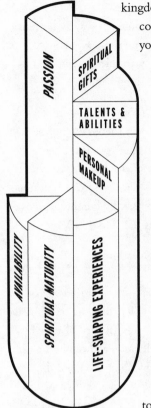

kingdom purposes. The combination of all of these components is the byproduct of how God made you.

The Bible says, "Just as each of us has one body with many members, and these members do not all have the same function, so in Christ we, though many, form one body" (Rom.12:4–5, TNIV). The Bible goes on to confirm that these components have been arranged in your life for the purposes of God according to His design and desire. "But in fact God has placed the parts in the body, every one of them, just as he wanted them to be" (1 Cor. 12:18, TNIV).

We will discuss the following major components in great detail in the coming chapters: passions, spiritual gifts, talents and abilities, personal make-up, life-shaping experiences, spiritual maturity, and availability. These components are different in every individual. Understanding them and incorporating them into everyday life are critical to living successful lives of purpose. These components come from three different sources: God, life's experiences, and our own personal choices.

## God-Shaping Factors

There are four main components to how God made you that come directly from Him and are woven into the fabric of your being:

- Passions
- Spiritual gifts
- Talents and abilities
- Personal makeup

Each of these areas will be defined and discussed in detail, and you will learn how they apply personally to your life in chapters 5 through 8.

## Life-Shaping Experiences

God also allows trials, tribulations, and tragedies to come our way as a means to help build character. The Bible is filled with great men and women who faced unbelievable, life-shaping experiences. Some were able to adjust something that was amiss in their life, or even to remove sinful habits.

Life-shaping experiences are often allowed by God (however, they are not always initiated by Him) to prepare and shape us. "Dear friends, do not be surprised at the fiery ordeal that has come on you to test you, as though something strange were happening to you. But rejoice inasmuch as you participate in the sufferings of Christ, so that you may be overjoyed when his glory is revealed" (1 Pet. 4:12–13, TNIV).

### Personal Choices and Disciplines

The level of our hunger and pursuit of spiritual things will determine our spiritual health, growth, and maturity. That's why the writer of Hebrews admonished those who were not living up to their full potential in Christ: "In fact, though by this time you ought to be teachers, you need someone to teach you the elementary truths of God's word all over again. You need milk, not solid food!" (Heb. 5:12, TNIV).

It is my prayer that these first four chapters have been instrumental in helping you understand what purpose is and bring you one step closer to becoming all God wants you to be. The next step on our journey is to define your purpose. The following seven chapters (Part Two) will outline each of the seven components that make you who you are. In the third part of the book you will learn how to put all of it into practice, resulting in a life that passionately fulfills the purpose of God! Self-discovery tools in Part Four are linked with each chapter.

In addition, our willingness to be used by God will ultimately determine the outcome of our lives. We can have all of the necessary God-given potential and gifting but still not be available. We should adopt Psalm 39:4–5 as our mindset for being available for Him: "Show me, Lord, my life's end and the number of my days; let me know how fleeting my life is. You have made my days a mere handbreadth; the span of my years is as nothing before you. Everyone is but a breath" (TNIV).

You are a child of God, created in His image, with certain characteristics that are yours alone. God knows your frame; He sees every part of your makeup and believes in your ability to measure up to the big plans He has for you. Regardless of your past or your present circumstances, you have a purpose to fulfill, and your uniqueness makes you the only one qualified to do so. You playing small does not serve the world. There is nothing enlightening about shrinking back so that other people won't feel insecure around you. You were born to make manifest the glory of God that is within you.

# PART TWO

## I AM WHAT I AM

CHAPTER FIVE

# LIVING THE DREAM
## LEARNING ABOUT YOUR PASSIONS

"[Not in your own strength] for it is God Who is
all the while effectually at work in you [energizing
and creating in you the power and desire], both to
will and to work for His good pleasure and
satisfaction and delight."

—Philippians 2:13, AMP

S ome people have all the amenities that come with a comfortable Westernized lifestyle: warm beds, clean water, dinner options, fashionable clothes, and two cars nestled snugly in a three-car garage. Others have none of these things.

In 1987 a wonderful friend of mine, Craig Fasler, went to Haiti for the first time. He thought he was familiar with the human condition, but he was about to get a crash course in the reality of lack, trekking through the northern jungle to a small village called Bonnet (pronounced bo-NET).

Imagine drawing water from a muddied river that has likely been contaminated upstream from free-range cattle, and bringing it back home for your children to drink. To Craig's revulsion, this was the reality of the people in this small village. When he learned this wasn't the exception, but rather the norm for five million of Haiti's eight million people,[1] his heart was rent.

Something happened during that trip that would revisit him years later in the middle of the night.

"The only way I could describe it is that it felt like God had turned my heart into a washcloth, and He was wringing it out," Craig remembers. "[That

39

experience] was significant to me, but somehow it got lost; you know how sometimes life gets back to usual and you forget.

"It was 1995 and I woke up in the middle of the night, and I heard this voice that said this simple phrase, 'What about the people of Bonnet?'"

The thought of millions of Haitians hiking at least two hours to retrieve fresh water sparked a curiosity in him about what it would take to dig a well in Bonnet. Craig couldn't get away from a consuming passion to see fresh water become available to these villagers. So he started saving money.

"I had a couple of missionary friends there named Richard Grubb and Rob Waters, and six months later I wired them $2,700 to put in the first well," he says.

Craig and his son, David, returned to Haiti in August that year and were disheartened to find an incomplete well about three feet in diameter. The people of Bonnet still didn't have the water they needed.

"It was so lined with rock that it would have ruined the drills they were using to dig the well," he says. "So they started lowering a man on a rope with a bucket fifty-five feet down this hole to chip away at the rock with a hammer. It was so frustrating to watch ... we just wanted there to be water in that well, but it was solid rock."

But the passion was still there. Craig and David returned home, bringing with them a chunk of rock from the well in progress. "We prayed over that rock every day."

In October, Craig received a message from Richard Grubb that would change his life: "They're drawing water out of the well in Bonnet."

Today (pending social and political challenges), Craig is on target to dig two wells a year in Haiti for the next twenty years.[2]

## What Is Passion?

Passion is consuming. It's tinged with discontent, restlessness, and determination that propel someone to action. And these are not necessarily unholy things (though they can be); within the context of pursuing godly purpose, consuming dissatisfaction can be the point at which you make the beautifully reckless decision to abandon yourself in pursuit of fulfilling your divine calling. But passion also has its effect on other causes. You don't have to go far before bumping into some.

There are those who are passionate about their careers, some to the point of sacrificing their own families in the wake of pursuing success.

Some are passionate about causes, such as political, environmental, or social issues. In fact, passion of the deepest, most dogmatic kind may drive some to follow these causes to the point of human destruction. We live in a world now shaken by the dubious acts of eco-terrorists, political tyrants, assassins, and terrorist thugs who've mishandled their impulses of passion to a sinister apex.

Passion, we can see, is one of mankind's most powerful driving forces. "All things have been created through him and for him" (Col. 1:16, TNIV), and that includes the passion He hard-wired within the heart of every person. But what does that mean specifically?

> **PASSION IS CONSUMING. IT'S TINGED WITH DISCONTENT, RESTLESSNESS, AND DETERMINATION THAT PROPEL SOMEONE TO ACTION.**

Passion can more simply be defined as a desire of the heart, given by God, that compels you to devote your resources and energy toward a specific area of interest or need, that makes a difference in the lives of others. It is a God-given internal guidance system for your motivation, desires, and inclinations that, once activated in service, will reap great satisfaction and fulfillment. Passion is a tool God has given you to help you achieve your purpose. It's what causes you to dream. It inspires you, it captivates your thoughts, it invades your emotions, and, in fact, it challenges you when you don't give it enough attention.

## Passion ... Directed

Ralph Waldo Emerson said quite poignantly, "A man is what he thinks about all day long."[3] What you are passionate about is the thing you have the greatest potential of becoming.

God intended passion to be all-consuming, "[Not in your own strength] for it is God Who is all the while effectually at work in you [energizing and creating in you the power and desire], both to will and to work for His good pleasure and satisfaction and delight" (Phil. 2:13, AMP). God intended all-consuming passion to be for His good pleasure

**WHAT YOU ARE PASSIONATE ABOUT IS THE THING YOU HAVE THE GREATEST POTENTIAL OF BECOMING.**

and delight. Passion is and must remain God-centered and God-focused.

So where is your passion focused? That passion you have for golf ... where is it leading you? What about your passion for success ... is it for God's good pleasure and delight, or your own?

Passion directed by God is an unstoppable force. But make no mistake, the devil conspires to arrest your passion and redirect it in other ways. Passion that doesn't have a clearly defined motive or regular monitoring of its effect has the potential to send anyone, even the most disciplined person, careening off course. This detour is, at minimum, a distraction and, in some cases, quite devastating.

How you direct your passion will greatly determine whether you are successful in fulfilling your purpose. Like a sharp knife in your kitchen drawer, passion can be extremely helpful or extremely harmful. It must be carefully directed and used for its intended purpose.

For many, being able to articulate a passion may be difficult, even though most of us have pursued our passions in some form or another. But have you ever taken time to define how God made you or to assess how your passions play a role in your overall makeup? The rest of this chapter will help you do just that. It will assist you in understanding four areas of passion, and then give you the opportunity to complete a personal passion assessment to identify the areas that excite and motivate you. Once you have defined your passions, we'll uncover how these passions apply to your purpose.

## Four Types of Passion

People tend to be passionate in four different ways: passion expressions, people passions, passions for certain issues, and passions for certain ministries.

### Passion Expressions

Passion expressions are simply the ways that you have been created to express what you're interested in. Each of us has things that really inspire us and things that really irritate us. For instance, I get really excited about strategizing, creating, and leading, but I have very little passion for maintaining those things.

There are many passion assessment tests available today. One of the more notable ones is found in Rick Warren's SHAPE materials. With the help of these tools, we can readily identify seventeen passion expressions. These are listed below but will be defined in detail in Part Four in your personal passion self-discovery exercise.

| | | |
|---|---|---|
| • Caring | • Intercession | • Performing |
| • Completing | • Leading & Overseeing | • Pioneering |
| • Creating | • Maintaining | • Repairing |
| • Designing | • Motivating | • Sharing or Giving |
| • Gathering | • Overcoming | • Strategizing |
| • Hospitality[4] | • Perfecting | |

You'll find these passions laced throughout almost every page of the Bible. Because passion is a God-given and God-intended resource, He chose to paint it upon the lives of every person in Scripture.

Take, for example, the prophet Anna, who was passionate about prayer. The Bible says, "She never left the temple but worshiped night and day, fasting and praying" (Luke 2:37, TNIV). We might feel good about an hour of prayer and an occasional day of fasting, but Anna did it night and day. Now that's passion!

Matthew had a passion for hospitality. He invited all of his tax-collecting buddies over to meet Jesus (Matt. 9:9–11). Paul was a passionate overcomer, persistently pushing through the most difficult of circumstances, including being whipped, robbed, stoned, imprisoned, lost at sea, and despised by friends (2 Cor. 11:24–29). What got him through all of this? A God-given passion to overcome, which he needed in order to fulfill his purpose. There was Abraham, Moses, Esther, and Ruth … the list goes on and on—people called by God, given certain passion expressions to fulfill God's will in their lives.

---

M y dentist and very close friend, Dr. Mark Jones, is perhaps the most passionate prayer warrior I have ever met. Over the course of our ten-year friendship, there has never been a time when he has not asked to pray for me when we meet, even in passing. You'll see him praying for people at leadership meetings and retreats; before, during, and after church services; or even when he's got you under local anesthetic in his dentist chair with a dozen instruments in your mouth. Have you ever tried to say, "Amen, brother!" with your numb mouth propped open? It sounds more like "Aaaaghh-graugh," but somehow the good doctor knows what you mean: "That's right; let that anointing settle deep down into your heart. Now move your tongue …" The guy is passionate about prayer!

---

### People Passions

God has placed particular people in your life whom you love being around. You might even be very passionate about spending time with them. These passions for people often align with the way you express your passion.

You may enjoy spending time with children, or you may like nothing more than to be around senior citizens. Some might enjoy visiting those in the hospital while others might really enjoy working with new believers. Each of us has different people passions, and they are placed in us to align with our purpose.

Jesus came "to seek and save what was lost," (Luke 19:10, TNIV); therefore, He was happy hanging out with sinners. Peter had a passion for the Jews, while Paul had a passion for the Gentiles. Over and over again, Scripture verifies that certain people get excited and focus their energies on particular types of people groups. Again, keep in mind that these people passions always aligned with their God-given purpose.

It would be impossible to identify every type of people group, but here are some common groups that appeal to people's passions within the context of serving:

| | | |
|---|---|---|
| • Infants | • Single Parents | • Prisoners |
| • Preschoolers | • Divorced | • Politicians |
| • Kindergartners | • Widowed | • Business People |
| • Elementary | • Senior Citizens | • Ethnic Groups |
| • Junior Highers | • Mentally Challenged | • Athletes |
| • High Schoolers | • Handicapped | • Military |
| • College | • Deaf | • Emergency Services |
| • Young Adults | • Blind | • Hospitalized |
| • Young Marrieds | • Poor | • Addictions |
| • Young Families | • Unemployed | • Spiritual Seekers |
| • Married Couples | • Homeless | • New Believers |

**Passion for Certain Issues**

The third area is passion directed toward certain issues. Have you ever noticed there are some who get excited about certain issues you never even knew existed? I used to feel bad about not being more passionate about other people's issues, but I began to realize that the reason other people were more passionate about them was that they were *supposed* to be! God made them to be geared that way, not me. Obviously this doesn't remove the responsibility to show compassion to all people in any circumstance, but it should minimize the unnecessary guilt you may have felt for not getting more involved in a particular issue.

Bruce Bugbee writes in his book *What You Do Best in the Body of Christ*:

The fact is, I can't care about everything equally. There are some things I care more about than others. That does not diminish the importance of any issue or concern. It simply means that my heart is drawn toward certain involvement. While I have compassion for the homeless, my passion leads me to make other commitments ... If we all cared about the same things, many of the needs in our world would go unmet. But God has put a divine magnet within each of us that is intended to attract us to the people, functions, or causes where he intends us to minister. This is not an afterthought on God's part. Our passion is built in to us so that we will conform ourselves to his purpose for our lives.[5]

The Bible shows people who have a passion for certain issues. Timothy was sent to many of the churches to disciple them in the ways of the Lord. Paul was passionate about church issues, as illustrated in both letters he wrote to church at Corinth. Esther had a passion for injustice, so she risked her life to stand up before the king on behalf of her people. David had a passion for politics and devoted himself to restoring the nation of Israel.

Just as there are too many people passions to mention, so it is with issues. Here are some common ones:

| | | |
|---|---|---|
| • Abortion | • Education | • Mental Health |
| • Abuse | • Environment | • Mentoring |
| • Addictions | • Family | • Politics |
| • Adoption | • Finance | • Poverty |
| • AIDS | • Health | • Racism |
| • Business | • Homosexuality | • Reaching the Lost |
| • Childcare | • Hunger | • Social Concerns |
| • Church | • Injustice | • Technology |
| • Disaster Relief | • International | • Violence |
| • Discipleship | • Literacy | |

After reading through the list, you might be able to quickly identify people you know who are passionate about one or more of these categories. Consider their dedication toward that particular issue and think back over your conversations with them. What do they talk about? Where do they spend their energy and money?

---

There are many issues that would never even raise my wife's eyebrow, but if you bring up the topic of young mothers, you might as well fire up the coffee pot, because this girl wants to chat! Susan has been wired with a passion for mentoring young mothers. She is currently involved in leading a thriving ministry called Moms with a Mission. She doesn't take a paycheck for what she does because Moms with a Mission is her passion. Susan spends countless hours in a given week, night and day, preparing Bible studies, praying with ladies, strategizing over the phone, and meeting with the leadership team—all because she has found her passion and purpose. The fulfillment in serving is rewarding for her.

---

**Passion for Specific Ministry Areas**

Finally, there are areas of ministry within any local church that always seem to draw certain people.

The Bible shows us individuals who were passionate about specific ministry areas. We refer to Philip as the evangelist and Paul as the apostle, serving in both form and function. Isaiah was a prophet. Solomon was involved in the ministry of leading. Read the book of Psalms and see why David was well known for his heart for worship ministry.

There are countless ministry opportunities in any given local church. Some larger churches have hundreds available. You should be able to list certain ministry areas that excite you.

---

A gifted young musician and anointed worship leader, Jeremy Scott has aligned and tapped into all four areas of passion. Jeremy has taken his passion and gifting for worship, youth, and discipleship and turned them into a full-fledged serving opportunity. He meets with a group of local young musicians every Saturday morning to raise them up in worship ministry as the next generation's worship leaders and musicians. Aside from working fifty hours or more per week at his job, Jeremy also leads worship frequently at his local church and recently married a beautiful woman who keeps his feet on the ground. And even with all of this going on, Jeremy's life is balanced and fulfilling because he has learned to eliminate time-wasting activities and focus on his passion. He gets up early on his day off every week and meets with a bunch of guys with guitars—that's passion!

## Discovering Your Personal Passions

Now is the time you've been waiting for, the moment of discovery. In order for this book to have the maximum impact in your life, I strongly suggest that you participate in the seven self-discovery tools found in Part Four. Each of these tools is linked to a specific chapter. **Turn to page 183 now and complete the personal passions exercise, "Defining Your Passions."** Then finish reading the last few pages of this chapter while it is fresh in your mind.

### Assessing Your Personal Passions

During your short self-discovery exercise, you should have been able to identify your top three Passion Expressions, People Passions, Issue Passions, and Ministry Passions. These are your passion strengths. Throughout this chapter you've seen certain examples of how these strengths have played out in the lives of various people. Take a moment and review your four areas of passions and ask yourself some questions:

• Is there a common thread that I see in all four categories?

• Have I identified any areas that reinforce something that I already knew or that someone has said about me in the past?

• Are there areas of ministry within my local church where my passions might be utilized?

• Is there something God has been speaking to me about lately that aligns with any of the passion areas I have identified?

## Serving with Discernment

Just like the old adage "There are two sides to every coin," passion also has two sides. If you are not careful, some of the dangers can cause as much harm as good. Let's briefly look at four cautionary things to consider:

**Your personal passions are only as valuable as the strength of your character.**
Passion is a wonderful gift from God. But keep in mind that it will tarnish if you lack the character quality needed to administrate it. It is imperative that we spend as much—if not more—time shaping our character as we do refining our passions. Paul admonishes the Galatian church to focus their passions and purpose through their character and not through their selfish ambitions and sinful desires. "But the fruit of the Spirit is love, joy, peace, patience, kindness, goodness, faithfulness, gentleness and self-control. Against such things there is no law" (Gal. 5:22–23, TNIV). Our

passions should always remain subservient to our character.

**Your personal passions are only one of many kingdom passions.**
You will always see your passion areas as most important. Why? Because
you're passionate about them! But what if nobody else is passionate about
those things? Learning to respect and champion other people's passions while
continuing to sharpen your own is a very delicate balance.

People are passionate about many different things. Thank God for that! Don't
be frustrated when others won't buy into giving their life to your cause.

**Your personal passions are not a personal excuse not to serve in
other areas.**
Serving must be our primary motive in all we do. I am a firm believer in pas-
sion-based ministry, but I am equally convinced that possessing the heart of
a servant and being willing to
serve wherever and whenever **SERVING MUST BE OUR PRIMARY**
is just as important. Never al- **MOTIVE IN ALL WE DO.**
low your passions and dedica-
tion to a particular area of serving to exclude you from the desire or responsibility to serve in other areas also. You can do both!

**Your personal passions are to be applied through the vision of the
local church.**
In God's infinite wisdom and plan, He designed the local church to be the instrument He uses to build and extend His kingdom and purposes. We're part
of that plan—how great is that? He has chosen each of us and placed within
us a specific purpose in a local church to fulfill His purposes. Your passions
and purpose are to assist Him in that. We are to build His church and not our
own ministries. If you keep this in mind, the vision of the local church will
never be in competition with your passions. The truth is your passions were
intended to build the local church.

At times, there might be some frustration because the local church and its
particular leadership might not emphasize or recognize areas that we are passionate about. This dilemma should never give any of us the license to build
our ministry in spite of our local church. Your passions and purpose were
designed specifically to fit like a jigsaw puzzle piece into the overall vision of
your church.

## Benefits to Serving with Your Passion Strengths

There are clear-cut benefits of serving with our passion strengths.

**Serving with your passion strengths can energize you!**
I often say to those who work with me, "If we can help people find their passion, they will give their lives to it." You won't have to motivate them; they will be energized on their own, serving in an area they really enjoy. Samuel Butler, the seventeenth-century author, said, "People are always good company when they are doing what they enjoy."[6] We all must be willing to serve anywhere there is a need, but our primary focus should remain serving in the area God created us to serve. You have identified your passions; now prayerfully consider how you can get more involved.

**Serving with your passion strengths can bring greater satisfaction and fulfillment.**
The main purpose for serving is others, as modeled by Jesus. He said, "For even I, the Son of Man, came here not to be served but to serve others" (Matt. 20:28, NLT). When you align your passions with your motivation to serve others, you receive the greatest satisfaction and fulfillment. By contrast, using your passion to build a name for yourself or to acquire some ministry title or position will always end in disappointment. The late comic George Burns once said, "I would rather be a failure doing something I love than a success doing something I hate."[7] Why? Because he understood that fulfillment is linked to passion. The years may wrinkle the skin, but serving long-term in areas outside of your passion will wrinkle the soul.

President Theodore Roosevelt said, "Far better is it to dare mighty things, to win glorious triumphs even though checkered by failure, than to rank with those poor spirits who neither enjoy nor suffer much because they live in the gray twilight that knows neither victory, nor defeat."[8] As you make serving others a daily pursuit and your primary motive in using your passion strengths, you will discover deep satisfaction and fulfillment like never before.

**Serving with your passion strengths can bring greater fruitfulness.**
People who focus their energies on their passion strengths will always be more fruitful. Tiger Woods' strength is golf. His name is synonymous with golf. He used a putter to learn to walk and began hitting a golf ball before the age of one. He was on the Mike Douglas show at age two, putting with Bob Hope. He

shot forty-eight for nine holes at age three and was featured in *Golf Digest* at age five. Imagine for a moment if Tiger Woods had focused his energy on quilting instead. It sounds silly, but people focus on things that are outside of their passion strengths all the time. And they are typically unfulfilled.

**Serving with your passion strengths can bring a greater sense of belonging and acceptance.**
Over the past twenty years, almost all of my best friendships have come from

Marcus Buckingham wrote a book called *Now, Discover Your Strengths,* which is focused entirely on this subject. In it he states, "Try to identify your strongest threads, reinforce them with practice and learning, and then either find or carve out a role that draws on these strengths every day. When you do, you will be more productive, more fulfilled, and more successful."[9]

those I have served with. We work and minister together, as well as play golf or go to a movie together. We have a deep sense of belonging in each other's company. Finding a place where you serve with someone of similar passions will open up a whole new world of camaraderie. Serving in your passion strengths will bring a greater sense of belonging and acceptance, resulting in deeper, more meaningful relationships with others.

**Serving with your passion strengths can bring personal growth and maturity.**
There is a famous saying: "Practice makes perfect." This applies to every area of life—playing an instrument, cooking, learning a sport, and sewing, to name a few. The more involved you are in a certain area, the more you'll grow. From a serving perspective, being involved in a ministry you enjoy will cause you to spend more of your time and energy focusing on kingdom thoughts, and the end result is excellence in that area. You will find yourself developing great character as well as honing your gifts and skills, which will result in spiritual health, growth, and maturity.

**WE ARE ONLY TRULY SUCCESSFUL WHEN OUR FOCUS IS KINGDOM SIGNIFICANCE.**

I may be stepping out on a limb here, but I firmly believe that you will never find true purpose and meaning in life unless you have engaged your passions in serving others. Just look at those in our culture who have spent their entire lives climbing the ladder of success, only to find out when they got there that they missed what was really important in life.

We are only truly successful when our focus is kingdom significance. When we shift from a success-driven mindset to a kingdom-significance mindset (and lifestyle), life's truest meaning is revealed, and we begin to really understand our purpose.

As you move forward discovering how God has made you, let your passions assist you. God has a dream for your life. Live it!

# CHAPTER SIX

# HOW'D I DO THAT? AND WHY?

## UNDERSTANDING YOUR SPIRITUAL GIFTS

> "We have many parts in the one body, and all
> these parts have different functions. In the same
> way, though we are many, we are one body in
> union with Christ, and we are all joined to each
> other as different parts of one body. So we are to
> use our different gifts in accordance with the grace
> that God has given us."
>
> —Romans 12:4–6, TEV

❝ You're going to hell, man!"

Sound callous? Maybe, but Ed Schefter had a message for his cohorts: turn or burn. He wasn't known for his subtlety as a college student, and he still isn't, though the years since have taught him a thing or two about temperance, the importance of being patient with others' life journeys, and understanding that delivering the Gospel compassionately is received much better than the old damnation battle cry.

At the time, however, he knew where his old gang was spiritually—he'd been there himself—but he also knew the inconceivable transformation that had taken place in his life. For some reason that he didn't understand at the time, he was stirred with a holy audacity to "tell it like it is" in hopes of persuading his friends to righteousness.

"I started doing dumb things at an early age," he explains. "I was smoking and stealing cigarettes when I was seven years old. My mom suffered from mental

53

illness and dad was a total workaholic ... I didn't feel a lot of acceptance at home, so I started hanging out with the wrong crowd.

"While all this was going on, my mom kept us attending a Presbyterian church, and when I was in junior high, I got involved in a church drama. Through that performance, I discovered something about drama and myself: I was hooked."

Acting came naturally to Ed. As a freshman in high school, he needed an English credit, so he took the easy route: drama class. Recognizing his talent and comfortable demeanor on stage, his teacher encouraged him to pursue acting as a career. Ed certainly had a gift for performance.

After high school, he enrolled in a local college and immersed himself in his theater studies. Ed's natural acting talent caught the attention of his professors, and they persuaded him to audition for acting schools. He followed their advice and was accepted to Cal Arts in Valencia, California. The real kicker came when Cal Arts offered him a full-ride scholarship.

Things looked promising for the prodigious young actor, but life wasn't without its hitches.

"I was doing more drugs and hanging out with more and more weird people," he says. "The whole theater crowd is pretty dark, for the most part. I was addicted to cocaine and doing every drug imaginable ... I realize now that if I'd continued down that road, I probably would have ended up dead.

"I remember one time having this 'burning bush' kind of experience. I was high on LSD and cocaine—I was a mess. I was driving and staring into the sun for the longest time, it must have been twenty minutes—I don't know how I stayed on the road. And I started to see this dark gray curtain coming down in front of me; it was like I was going blind. I thought I'd done damage to my retinas, or worse. I cried out, 'Lord, if You're there ...' and I told Him everything I'd done—like He didn't know—and I said 'I'll serve You, just don't let me go blind!' Suddenly, that curtain just totally disappeared."

That experience left Ed knowing something had to change in his life. Somewhere between all he had to anticipate and all he had to regret was a point of reckoning, an intersection where he had to make some decisions. Forecasting the result of continuing down the same path wasn't rocket science. He knew what he had to do: keep his end of the bargain with God.

A couple of months went by, and there was a sudden death in Ed's family. At the funeral "my brother and sister knew what I was up to, and they confronted me about the choices I'd made and the lifestyle I was living. It got me thinking about things even more." So on Thanksgiving Day in 1979, Ed responded to the gentle tug on his heart and gave his life to Christ.

"It rocked my world," he says, describing his powerful conversion. "I'd never experienced anything like it—no drug, no high could compare. My self-centered passions couldn't compare to knowing God. I went back to my friends in this very extreme way and told them, 'You're going to hell, man!'—which I realize now wasn't the best thing to say, but I had to say *something*.

"I needed to separate myself from that whole way of life, and I knew God was telling me to drop out of school. It wasn't even a decision for me; I knew I'd be a fool not to respond!"

Ed packed up the textbooks he'd just shelled out $500 for, toted them to school, and gave them back. In a single afternoon he dropped out of school and forfeited his opportunity to attend Cal Arts the following year, boldly stepping out of his own plan and into the purpose of God.

In the twenty-some years that followed, Ed went to Bible college and devoted his life to serving the church. In 1996, at the request of his pastor, Ed penned a dramatic presentation he simply called *Eternity*. It's a sequence of heaven and hell vignettes that portray the eternal significance of one's acceptance or denial of the gift of salvation. *Eternity* was so successful that requests came pouring in from other churches that wanted to host the production as well.

To this day, *Eternity* is still going strong. An estimated 2.3 million people have seen the production around the globe—Singapore, Australia, South Africa, New Zealand, the United States, and Canada—resulting in more than 250,000 documented salvations.

"The heart and soul of the *Eternity* production isn't the dramatic aspect, but seeing people saved and assimilated into a local church. Evangelism is what it's all about."[1]

---

## T-Boned by God on the Highway of Life

There comes a point when each of us is confronted with God's specific plan for us, which usually differs greatly from our own. There we are, cruising down the highway of life trying to build a life for ourselves, when we're suddenly, massively, and miraculously T-boned by the Creator of the universe, who presents us with a choice: continue traveling toward our own formulated destination or make the necessary, life-changing course adjustments to follow His plan.

This usually happens when our dreams and desires (our will) intersect with God's plans and purposes (His will). Those who make the decision to align their life with God's will can be assured the blessed opportunity for more similar choices throughout life's journey. In fact, generally about the time we think we've made it successfully through one life-changing encounter, we can start to see the next signal approaching and wonder what "adjustment" awaits us up ahead. You don't have to be a Christian long to realize that life is a series of these intersections, each one presenting another opportunity to exchange our own dreams and desires for God's perfect plan and amazing purpose. The rewards, however, are out of this world.

If you're like most people, this can be overwhelming. To be encountered by the Creator of the universe with the news that He knew you before even one speck of this world had been created, and that He chose you, giving you a specific purpose, can render you speechless.

Many simply discount these supernatural encounters, unaware of their potential to drive through life at a blazing speed like a svelte performance automobile. Instead of realizing they were engineered for high performance, they buy into the deception that God created them to be cheap, junky, and gutless, tooling down life's highway going absolutely nowhere.

The reality is, God intends your journey in life to be laced with intersections that are frequent and sometimes overwhelming. He wants to confront the "ordinary" perspective you may have of yourself with His unbelievable plan for your life. He wants to take you on a wild ride, a journey that's meant to be exhilarating! In these moments, God will show you three significant realities about your life and purpose.

First, He will show you that His plan for your life is larger than you could ever imagine. "By his mighty power at work within us, he is able to accomplish infinitely more than we would ever dare to ask or hope" (Eph. 3:20, NLT). He confronts us daily with the idea that whatever we consider our purpose to be is too small!

Second, He wants to imbed into your self-awareness something very important—that this great vision He has for you cannot and will not be accomplished by

**THIS GREAT VISION HE HAS FOR YOU CANNOT AND WILL NOT BE ACCOMPLISHED BY YOU ON YOUR OWN.**

you on your own. Jesus made this clear when He said, "Yes, I am the Vine; you are the branches. Whoever lives in me and I in him shall produce a large crop of fruit. For apart from me you can't do a thing" (John 15:5, TLB). In Matthew 19:26, He said, "But with God all things are possible" (TNIV). Jesus was implying in these two accounts that whoever lives for Him should have great purpose and live a very fruitful, abundant life. But He is quick to point out that none of us will ever be able to reach our destination if He is not the central focus of our lives.

Third, He wants you to know He's given you a specially designed set of divine tools, which will help you as you head toward your destination. These tools are called spiritual gifts. With these, you'll come to understand that only with His assistance and by placing total trust in Him will your purpose be accomplished.

Paul explained to the church at Corinth that "a spiritual gift is given to each of us as a means of helping the entire church" (1 Cor. 12:7, NLT). Every believer has been given spiritual gifts, and God intends that we use them as primary tools in accomplishing His supernatural plan for our lives. He also said that "we are to use our different gifts in accordance with the grace that God has given us" (Rom. 12:6, TEV). Even Jesus Himself, in every recorded ministry situation, relied on the gifts of the Holy Spirit, showing us the necessity of using spiritual gifts as the sole means of fulfilling purpose.

George Barna conducted a study in 2001 that found that 29 percent of Christian adults have never even heard of the concept of spiritual gifts, while 69 percent have heard of it but don't know what their spiritual gifts might be.[2]

## What Are Spiritual Gifts?

One of the most important truths we can seek to understand is the value and proper use of our spiritual gifts. This is instrumental in directing us toward fulfilling our purpose and becoming who God created us to be. A spiritual gift is a divine attribute given to someone by the Holy Spirit, according to God's grace, at conversion; it is to be used for building up the body of Christ and ministering to others.

In other words, the moment you decided to give your life to Christ, He placed within you specific gifts with the intention that you would use them to make your life count … serving others, building up the local church, and reaching your world for Christ. He wants you to use your spiritual gifts. Ignoring them may result in constant frustration, lack of spiritual fulfillment, and a crippled destiny.

---

There was a man named Edgar who lived most of his life on the streets of Brooklyn. Poor old Edgar spent his days rummaging through trash cans behind restaurants, hoping to score a few scraps for a meal. He gathered aluminum cans and plastic bottles to recycle for a few cents and panhandled for strangers' compassion as a way to make ends meet. Sometimes he'd use the day's "proceeds" to buy a can of dog food … a cheaper meal than other items on grocery store shelves. At night Edgar would make his way back to the basement of a condemned building, where there was no running water or electricity, just a few gutter rats that had become his only friends. This was the place he called home, where he would lay his head on the cold concrete floor and fall asleep, only to begin the hopeless process again the next day.

One cold winter night, Edgar froze to death in his lonely abode. After a few days, city workers found his body and, after digging through his personal belongings, located the addresses of his two grown children.

The funeral was short and simple. Few people attended, few tears were shed.

Edgar's lonely existence was finally over. Afterward, the man's children stopped by to pick up his few belongings: some clothes, a pocketknife, a hat, one glove … and a box containing a large rock, given as a gift by an anonymous person, that Edgar had used to prop the door open to his cold urban cavern. Intrigued by the uniqueness of this rock, his children took it to a geologist friend, who pointed out to their utter amazement that this was one of the largest uncut diamonds ever discovered … worth a staggering $12 million!

Edgar lived a hard life struggling to survive out on the streets. Then one day his life was over, and he never realized that the rock he kicked up against the door every day was the key to changing his life forever. Within his reach had been a special gift that would have changed everything. Imagine how his life might have changed if he had recognized his doorstop for what it truly was and discovered its worth.[3]

## Types of Spiritual Gifts

Every Christian has been given one or more spiritual gifts. These gifts vary from person to person. Although many people share similar gifts and gift mixes, God has placed specific gifts in each of us that enable us to do all that He has called us to do.

Many people have varying ideas as to the number of spiritual gifts identified in the Bible. Some believe there are as few as seven gifts available to today's Christian, while others believe there are as many as twenty-six.

As for me and the leaders of the local church where I serve, we've concluded that there are eighteen. (See page 193 for their definitions and scriptural references for your review. Try to identify which ones are already operating in your life.)

- Administration/Ruling
- Apostle/Pioneer
- Discernment
- Evangelism
- Exhortation
- Faith
- Giving
- Healing
- Helps/Serving

- Interpretation
- Knowledge
- Mercy

- Miracles
- Pastor/Shepherd
- Prophecy

- Teaching
- Tongues
- Wisdom

## The Purposes of Spiritual Gifts

The purposes of spiritual gifts are as numerous as the needs of the Church, both inside (pastoral) and outside (evangelistic). Whenever we're called upon to partner with God in touching the lives of others in any form or fashion, spiritual gifts are engaged. Certain gifts you will utilize regularly, while others you may only tap into on rare occasions. Regardless of how many or how few, our focus must always be to use our gifts consistently with their designed purpose. Purposes of spiritual gifts include the following:

**To bring glory to God.**
The goal of everything we do, including the use of spiritual gifts, is to bring glory to God. "Whatever you do, work at it with all your heart, as working for the Lord, not for human masters" (Col. 3:23, TNIV). There should never be a time when we use spiritual gifts to build a name for ourselves or to pursue some platform or position. Jesus said, "For I seek not to please myself but him who sent me" (John 5:30, TNIV). This one purpose must be at the forefront every time we use our gifts.

**To confirm God's Word.**
The use of spiritual gifts will never contradict God's Word and its truths, only confirm it further. In every account in the Bible where a spiritual gift is used, you'll find a truth being reinforced. God's Spirit, His Word, and the use of spiritual gifts in your life must be consistent!

While I don't want to devote a great deal of time to discussing theological views of spiritual gifts, there are many well-written books available today that will provide everything you need to form your own conclusions. Here are five recommended titles:

1. *The Church in the New Testament* by Kevin J. Conner

2. *Discover Your Spiritual Gifts* by C. Peter Wagner

3. *Spiritual Gifts* by Bryan Carraway

4. *Discover Your Spiritual Gifts the Network Way* by Bruce L. Bugbee

5. *Ministering Through Spiritual Gifts* (The In Touch Study Series) by Charles Stanley

Someone once told a pastor friend of mine that he felt he had permission to leave his wife because he prayed that, as a confirmation from God, all the signals would turn green on his way to work. Coincidentally, every signal that day turned green, which meant he was justified to commit adultery.

I don't care if every light *on the entire planet* turned green at the same time; this would never constitute justification for sin. It contradicts God's Word.

**To build up others, not yourself.**
Jesus Himself came to serve, not to be served (Matt. 20:28). He recognized that everything in life is not only to bring glory to God, but to bring glory to God by serving others. This may be a simple concept to define, but a difficult one to live out. The famous D.L. Moody said, "The measure of a man is not in how many servants he has, but how many men he serves."[4] Peter confirmed these life principles by admonishing, "Each of you should use whatever gift you have received to serve others, as faithful stewards of God's grace in its various forms" (1 Pet. 4:10, TNIV). As you set your hearts on using your spiritual gifts, let your focus be serving others.

**To empower you for supernatural works.**
Each of us is a supernatural being with a temporary natural experience—not the other way around. The natural world in which we live is temporary, while the kingdom of God is primarily spiritual and supernatural. That doesn't mean we've been given license to neglect or deny the fact that there is a natural world, but it should provoke us to remember that we will never accomplish supernatural acts without the assistance of spiritual gifts.

---

A my Dodson developed cancerous tumors in her left leg when she was ten years old. She made it through her teenage years, but by the time she turned nineteen, doctors had to amputate her leg. At age twenty-two she lost her left lung to the same disease. What's so inspiring about Amy's life is that from her earliest childhood memories, she envisioned herself running marathons. With the removal of her left leg, however, this dream would have to be left in the fantasy file.

A few years later, Amy was chosen to be the benefactor of a new technology that would allow her to have a special prosthetic leg, which enabled her to fulfill her childhood dream. On October 5, 2002, at forty years old, Amy ran 26.2 miles in just under four hours, breaking Lindsay Nielsen's record for a woman leg-amputee by twenty-four minutes and thirteen seconds. As if that weren't enough, she did it at the Saint George Marathon in Utah, a course several-thousand feet above sea level that includes a steep climb up the side of a volcano.[5]

If not for medical technology, Amy's inability to accomplish her childhood ambition would have left her in a place of frustration. This gift enabled her not only to realize her dream, but also to far exceed anyone's expectations!

---

Without the use of spiritual gifts, our ambitions to accomplish supernatural works would limp along in frustration. It is a fantasy to expect the supernatural to flow out of a natural gift.

For many years, I've served closely with a group of men and women who have given their lives to the local church. One of the benchmark statements our team has embraced is, "What I'm a part of is more important than the role I play." We've been able to accomplish a great deal more as a team than any of us could ever have accomplished on our own.

Such is the case with you. What you're part of is more important than the role that you play. In other words, using your spiritual gifts to serve the local church is more important than merely having spiritual gifts and using them unintentionally.

We see this principle illustrated at the dawn of the first-century Church. The very first thing they were instructed to do was to go to an upper room and wait. While they waited, a gift was imparted to them. Jesus promised, "You will receive power when the Holy Spirit comes on you" (Acts 1:8, TNIV). That's exactly what happened—the Holy Spirit moved, and supernatural things happened!

It is interesting to see the immediate change in the disciples' lives when they recognized and received this profound revelation. Look at Peter's life. This is the guy who, just a few weeks earlier, was labeled the spineless wonder! Three times he denied Christ (Luke 22:54–62). His natural means brought frustration and very little fruit. But a few weeks later, after his encounter with the Holy Spirit, he was exercising his newfound spiritual gifts and saw three thousand people saved!

**To partner with the ministry of the Holy Spirit.**
I am amazed at how easily I can lose sight of the reason why I serve. It's probably just as easy for you too. Come on, be honest … how many times a week do you have to challenge your thinking and calibrate your reason for serving with the purpose God has for your life? We are here to accomplish *His* purpose; He is not here to assist us in accomplishing *our* purpose. I find during my prayer times that I often have to go back to the same old prayer: "Lord, help me to assist You in doing Your thing … I cannot expect You to assist me in accomplishing my own thing."

Eugene Peterson so eloquently articulates the words of our Savior

**WE ARE HERE TO ACCOMPLISH HIS PURPOSE; HE IS NOT HERE TO ASSIST US IN ACCOMPLISHING OUR PURPOSE.**

regarding the promise of the Holy Spirit to guide us and lead us in all we do. "I will talk to the Father, and he'll provide you another Friend so that you will always have someone with you. This Friend is the Spirit of Truth. The godless world can't take him in because it doesn't have eyes to see him, doesn't know what to look for. But you know him already because he has been staying with you, and will even be *in* you!" (John 14:16–17, MSG).

**To build up your local church.**
I firmly believe that the local church is God's instrument for bringing hope to the world. The apostle Paul clearly explained that spiritual gifts were used to build up the local church. He said, "A spiritual gift is given to each of us as a means of helping the entire church" (1 Cor. 12:7, NLT).

The Church is referred to in Scripture as "the body of Christ." Each of us has been created to be a part of that body. Paul continued, "You can easily enough see how this kind of thing works by looking no further than your own body. Your body has many parts—limbs, organs, cells—but no matter how many parts you can name, you're still one body. It's exactly the same with Christ. By means of his one Spirit, we all said good-bye to our partial and piecemeal lives. We each used to independently call our own shots, but then we entered into a large and integrated life in which *he* has the final say in everything" (1 Cor. 12:12–13, MSG).

### To bring freedom to the bound.

Your spiritual gifts are not just a metaphor for the Church and her splendor, but an essential part in fulfilling that which God intended the Church to be, including her rule over principalities and powers. In chapter 3, we looked at the fourfold purpose of man, which is the foundation of our individual purpose. As we move forward in our purpose, we will be consistently confronted with an enemy who is like a roaring lion seeking to devour us and others.

### To comfort the afflicted and afflict the comforted.

Jesus always had a way with words and was never caught off guard, even in the most difficult circumstances. His secret was total reliance on the Holy Spirit and dependency on spiritual gifts. In each of the 199 recorded ministry situations involving Jesus, you'll find Him using one or more spiritual gifts.[6] In one case, Jesus is talking with a group of people when a woman caught in the act of adultery is thrown at His feet (John 8:1–11). Here in this amazing account we see Jesus using the gifts of discernment, wisdom, and words of knowledge to bring comfort to the afflicted (the woman) and in the same breath, affliction to the comforted (the Pharisees).

**YOUR LIFE HAS PURPOSE, AND IT'S MEANT TO EXTEND BEYOND THE FOUR WALLS OF YOUR OWN LIFE AND BEYOND THE ROSE-COLORED, STAINED-GLASS WINDOWS OF YOUR CHRISTIAN CULTURE.**

Every one of us knows someone or has had an encounter with someone who is either afflicted or too proud to be comfortable. Part of finding our purpose and fulfilling it is to make a difference in the lives of these people. It is comforting to know that, if we just ask the Holy Spirit to help us in these difficult circumstances, He will give us words of wisdom and discernment to change the course of their lives.

### To bring salvation.

Your life has purpose, and it's meant to extend beyond the four walls of your own life and beyond the rose-colored, stained-glass windows of your Christian culture. There are billions of people who desperately need Christ. Our responsibility is to extend God's kingdom, leading lost people to salvation. This may seem overwhelming, but it is part of your purpose! The exciting part is that God has given you everything you need (spiritual gifts) to succeed.

Like most other areas of life, when we focus on our own inadequacies, we fall short of obtaining our goal. So it is with reaching the unchurched. Remember, apart from God, we can't do a single thing. Only when we realize that He has equipped us with divine tools, focusing on what He can do through us, will we be able to affect the nations! This challenge is solidified in John 20: "Jesus performed many other signs in the presence of his disciples, which are not recorded in this book. But these are written that you may believe that Jesus is the Messiah, the Son of God, and that by believing you may have life in his name" (John 20:30–31, TNIV).

Hopefully, each of us lives a relatively full and free life–this is the launching pad to making a difference in the lives of those around us every day. Most of them are likely bound by addictions, bad habits, hurts, and offenses that may have festered for years. We will never be able to help set people free without using our spiritual gifts. The Bible reminds us, "For though we live in the world, we do not wage war as the world does. The weapons we fight with are not the weapons of the world. On the contrary, they have divine power to demolish strongholds" (2 Cor. 10:3-4, TNIV).

## Finding Your Spiritual Gifts

In the previous chapter, you were asked to take a few minutes and personally identify the passions God has placed in your life. Now you'll have the opportunity to do the same regarding your spiritual gifts. You can identify your spiritual gifts through the self-discovery exercises in Part Four of this book.

**Please turn to page 187. You'll find a self-discovery exercise ("Identifying Your Spiritual Gifts") with more information.** Once you've finished, return to this page and continue reading.

## Concerns Regarding Your Spiritual Gifts

Cautiously and prayerfully consider the following concerns about the discovery and development of your spiritual gifts.

**Don't exalt one gift above another; all gifts are equally important.** Unfortunately, today's society has done a good job of elevating certain individuals who have a public platform. This has also permeated the Church. The reality is that God sees the gift of teaching, which may be used to equip thousands, as equally important as the gift of serving in children's ministry. Whatever gifts you have, they are vitally important to God!

## Understanding Your Spiritual Gifts

The self-discovery exercises will begin a process that will continue for a lifetime. Just understanding a little bit more about how God made you should encourage you to begin applying these to your purpose and passion areas. Here are some considerations regarding the results of your spiritual gifts assessment:

• This exercise is only a tool and not the final authority regarding spiritual gifts in your life.

• The length of your Christian walk and the depth of your spiritual maturity will factor into the accuracy and relevancy of this exercise.

• Get some feedback from leaders you respect, asking them how the results might apply to your life and circumstances.

• Realize that acknowledgment of certain gifts doesn't automatically give you the platform or license to begin functioning in any specific area of ministry.

• Recognize the gifts identified may be in an embryonic form and may take years to develop fully.

**Glorify the gift Giver, not the gift user.**

Remember, it is God—and God alone—working in the lives of people that makes them great stewards of spiritual gifts. Paying awe to the gift user, rather than the gift Giver, can deceive us as to who really deserves the glory. God brings the increase, the blessing, and the influence. Make sure that your focus is always on the Giver, not the user or even the gifts themselves.

**Don't confuse spiritual gifts with passions or natural talents.**

We learned about passions in the previous chapter and will learn more about natural talents and abilities in the following chapter. Although there may be some similarities between these personal attributes, they are vastly different from spiritual gifts.

**Elevate the importance of the fruit of the Spirit over the gifts of the Spirit.**

Paul addressed some concerns taking place in the church at Corinth regarding the over-inflated importance and misuse of spiritual gifts (1 Cor. 13:1–7). In chapter 12 he let the church know that the gifts are important but concluded with a powerful statement: "But now I want to lay out a far better way for you" (1 Cor. 12:31, MSG). He then compared the gifts of the Spirit with the fruits of the Spirit, emphasizing that gifts without character mean nothing.

He reiterated this point later: "Go after a life of love as if your life depended upon it—because it does. Give yourselves to the gifts God gives you" (1 Cor. 14:1, MSG). Paul presented the balance: set your hearts on living a life of great character while you use your spiritual gifts to fulfill your purpose.

- Experiment with your gifts through serving. Put them to use!

- Take some time to meditate upon your passions and gifts and see how the two can work together in serving in your local church.

**Don't assume that your gifts will remain vibrant without use.**
Anyone who spends time at the gym has seen probably seen that one dedicated guy who is there all the time, and you can't help but admire his beautifully ripped muscles that he has worked so hard to build. Then there's me, who, after one set of curls (with a ten-pound weight), expects to see some profound difference in my physique. The reality is, if I'm going to see any results, I must frequent the gym.

So it is with spiritual gifts. Spiritual maturity belongs to those who practice using their spiritual gifts often. If you don't use them, they won't grow! The writer of Hebrews said, "Milk is for beginners, inexperienced in God's ways; solid food is for the mature, who have some practice in telling right from wrong" (Heb. 5:14, MSG). The word *practice* in this verse is actually translated from the original Greek word *gumnazo*, which means "to exercise or to train" (it's also where we get the English word *gymnasium*). Thus, if you want to fully develop in your Christian walk, you must exercise your gifts in the daily gymnasium of life. Lack of use produces flabby results.

**"GO AFTER A LIFE OF LOVE AS IF YOUR LIFE DEPENDED UPON IT-BECAUSE IT DOES. GIVE YOURSELVES TO THE GIFTS GOD GIVES YOU."**
-PHILIPPIANS 1:20-21, MSG

## Benefits of Using Your Spiritual Gifts
Spiritual gifts bring great blessings to those who embrace and use them often. You can be guaranteed that as you focus on your purpose, ignite your passions, and use your spiritual gifts, these benefits will be yours for the taking.

**You will be a better Christian as you live your life for Him.**
The more you focus on fulfilling your purpose and using your gifts, the less

time and interest you will have on those things that bring no eternal reward.

**You will find true satisfaction serving in an area where you are gifted.**
I have applied to my own life what I call "the 80/20 rule." That means 80 percent of my time should be devoted to those areas of service I am most passionate about and spiritually gifted in; 20 percent of my time should be devoted to serving in other areas of need, which may require a greater measure of self-discipline.

**You will have a sense of greater significance as you apply your gifts toward building the local church.**
As you get involved in serving God's glorious bride (the Church), you will feel a sense of indescribable significance. Realizing you are part of God's eternal plan and that He has passed the baton to you will strengthen your heart to run the race with even more vigor.

> SPIRITUAL MATURITY BELONGS TO THOSE WHO PRACTICE USING THEIR SPIRITUAL GIFTS OFTEN.

**You will have a deeper sense of fulfillment as your gifts bring glory to God.**
When you have identified your purpose and passions, defined your spiritual gifts, and integrated them into your daily life, you will find great fulfillment knowing that it brings glory to God.

**You will receive greater eternal rewards for faithfully using your spiritual gifts.**
There will come a time when each of us will stand before the throne of God. He will ask, "What did you do with the gifts and talents you received?" What will you say? Will there be a list of exciting accomplishments, or will your mind scramble for an excuse?

We are all faced with the same dilemma every morning when we lift our head from our pillow: what will we do today to accomplish our God-intended purpose? Tomorrow, you can wake up knowing that you have been given another piece of the equation of finding and fulfilling your purpose. Along with your passions, you have been adorned with the supernatural deposit of spiritual gifts as a means to fulfilling your purpose. The choice to use them is yours.

CHAPTER SEVEN

# SECOND NATURE
## DEFINING YOUR TALENTS AND ABILITIES

> "But in fact God has placed the parts in the body,
> every one of them, just as he wanted them to be."
>
> —1 Corinthians 12:18, TNIV

**M**illard Fuller had ambition and then some. His personal aspiration to make $10 million seemed feasible, considering he possessed natural talents and abilities rarely seen in men his age. By the time he was thirty, he had earned his first million, which came with all the accoutrements you'd expect with the millionaire lifestyle of a talented young businessman. Millard enjoyed the satisfaction of knowing that he had arrived at successes typical of men nearly twice his age. Affluence left a sweet taste in his mouth.

And sharp pains in his chest.

Millard's heart attack came unexpectedly—not the type involving clogged arteries, but the kind of medical emergency brought on in the midst of clogged priorities. Though his empire was rising, Millard's marriage and family had been eroding away at the same rapid pace as his health. About that time, his wife Linda, disenchanted with not being one of Millard's ten million ambitions, announced that she no longer loved him and would be leaving for New York City with their children to confer with a minister friend regarding her options. She wanted more. She wanted a husband.

"The week that followed was the loneliest, most agonizing time in my life," Millard says, remembering how his talents, abilities, and lofty ambitions seemed to replace everything he truly cared about. "I forgot to add meaning and purpose to my life plan."

Out of desperation, he called his wife and begged her to see him. Linda was reluctant, but she agreed, and Millard jumped on the very next plane to New York.

Over the next few days and weeks, God began to restore their marriage, mission, and purpose in life. Together they strategized how to allow God to use their talents and resources for His purpose and plans, and were able to identify what mattered most in their lives.

Stepping out on a limb, Millard and Linda sold everything and donated all the proceeds to their church and some colleges and charities. They walked away from their millionaire lifestyle, deeper in love with each other and with life. Millard's friends thought he'd gone crazy, but he couldn't have felt saner. The rest of his days would be committed to applying his talents and abilities to the purpose he knew was from God.

Clarity for Millard and Linda came during a visit with Clarence Jordan, a theologian in overalls. Clarence had started a Christian community called Koinonia near the small southwest Georgia town of Americus. He showed Millard the dilapidated shacks that lined the dirt roads of the surrounding countryside. These tumbledown shanties, which often leaked from the rain and lacked heat and plumbing, were home to hundreds of impoverished families. Millard knew that if 25 percent of the world's population lived in substandard housing (or none at all), that meant almost 1.4 billion people lived like this.

Millard was stirred with compassion to help in some way, but he wasn't sure how. He was confident that he had the ability to do something, but all he could think of was to start building.

Before the first house was completed, Clarence died of a heart attack. Moved by Clarence's compassion to make a difference in the lives of impoverished people everywhere and by the overwhelming gratitude of those who received new homes, Millard packed up his family and set off for Zaire, where they devoted the next three years to building homes for needy people. Eventually, they returned to Georgia, where, in 1976, Millard and Linda Fuller launched a little organization called Habitat for Humanity.

Millard, who once used his talents in pursuit of his $10 million goal, realized that God had given him a vision to use those same talents and abilities to build ten million homes. Their mission was simple: "Everyone who gets sleepy at night should have, at the very least, a simple, decent, affordable place to lay their heads."

Through the work of Habitat for Humanity, thousands of income-deficient families have found new hope in the form of affordable housing. Churches, community groups, Hollywood elite, and others—even former President Jimmy Carter—have joined together to successfully tackle a significant social challenge: suitable housing for all. Today, Habitat for Humanity has built more than 200,000 homes, sheltering more than one million people in more than 3,000 communities worldwide.[1]

---

## What Is a Talent?

Have you ever been amazed at the extraordinary talent of a professional athlete? Every time I see that famous video clip of Michael Jordan single-handedly slamming the ball, virtually from half court, mouth open wide and fire in his eyes, I am amazed. To him, that stunt is second nature. He was born with a unique talent for basketball.

Imagine any one of these amazing singers—Andrea Bocelli, Sarah Brightman, Celine Dion, Luciano Pavarotti—whose vocal ranges cover four or five octaves and who can woo the masses. If I'm really lucky (and the shower acoustics are just right), I *might* get three to four notes to be on key. That's because I have a special talent of consistently singing *off* key. Pavarotti might be able to shatter a glass with his high notes, but can he attract every stray dog in the neighborhood and get them to howl simultaneously?

The truth is, you could choose any area of culture and quickly identify champions at the top of their game. What these people have in common is that they have recognized their talents, developed them, and focused their lives on utilizing them for maximum impact.

What are the talents God has given you? Recent studies show that the average

Webster's Dictionary defines talent as "a natural endowment or ability of a superior quality." My own definition is: "A unique skill or ability imbedded within the core of your being, designed to be used in fulfilling your God-intended purpose, that enables you to excel in a specified area."

person has between five hundred and seven hundred talents operable in his or her life. Some may be stronger than others and will rise to the surface as predominant life talents. Nonetheless, you have been wired with plenty of talents that make you more than capable of fulfilling your God-intended purpose.

Unlike spiritual gifts, which are deposited supernaturally into our being at conversion, most talents are woven into our DNA. Some skills may be acquired through the application of knowledge and experience following birth, but even those are nothing more than mere complements of those talents established in our genetic code.

In his book *Now, Discover Your Strengths*, Marcus Buckingham expounded upon this profound concept.

> Forty-two days after you are conceived, your brain experiences a four-month growth spurt. Actually, the word 'spurt' doesn't do justice to the sheer scale of what happens. On your forty-second day you create your first neuron, and 120 days later you have a hundred billion of them. That's a staggering 9,500 neurons being created every second. But once this explosion slows down, much of the neuron drama is over. You have a hundred billion when you are born, and you have about that many up until late middle age ... Sixty days before your birth, your neurons start trying to communicate with one another. Each neuron literally reaches out a strand called an axon and attempts to make a connection ... during the first three years of your life, your neurons prove phenomenally successful at making these connections. In fact, by the age of three each of your hundred billion neurons has formed 15,000 synaptic connections with other neurons. Just to be clear, that is 15,000 connections for *each* of your hundred billion neurons.[2]

Because of these connections, you begin to develop certain behavior patterns pertaining to your skills and abilities from the moment you are born. At your earliest age, you recognize there are some things you are good at and others you're not so good at. As you continue to grow, you tend to lean toward those things at which you are more skilled and avoid those that are more challenging and may make you feel inferior. This begins the process of setting you on a course, developing certain areas in your life more than others, forming recognizable talents and abilities. Over the childhood and adolescent years, your body begins to sever those connections that aren't being used, and by the time you are sixteen, more than half of your mental network is shut down. Those connections that remain will create certain strengths, which we know as "talents" that seem to come easy to us. As time progresses, these things can become second nature.

God has given each of us some very specific talents, and He wants us to use them! These talents were intricately designed into the fiber of your being and are natural tools that give you the ability to achieve your purpose. Your passions are like the motor that gets you going in the right direction, and your talents help you to do a good job along the way. Your spiritual gifts give you an extra boost, as God gives you supernatural assistance to do it all with excellence. All of these work together in harmony to help you reach your specific goal.

## Types of Talents

Throughout the Scriptures, we can see how God used certain people with certain talents for specific seasons. Although we don't have the privilege of being able to dissect the personal makeup of every biblical figure, there are plenty of examples of God using people's talents in order to fulfill purpose.

**YOUR SPIRITUAL GIFTS GIVE YOU AN EXTRA BOOST, AS GOD GIVES YOU SUPERNATURAL ASSISTANCE TO DO IT ALL WITH EXCELLENCE. ALL OF THESE WORK TOGETHER IN HARMONY TO HELP YOU REACH YOUR SPECIFIC GOAL.**

One of the greatest examples is found in the Old Testament. God asked Moses to build the Tabernacle. Based on God's expectation and detailed blueprint, this would be no small task. Where would Moses find the right people? Well, in God's infinite wisdom, He placed certain people in Moses' path who were created with a specific purpose and a special set of talents to finish the job and do it well.

Then the Lord said to Moses, "See, I have chosen Bezalel son of Uri, the son of Hur, of the tribe of Judah, and I have filled him with the Spirit of God, with wisdom, with understanding, with knowledge and with all kinds of skills—to make artistic designs for work in gold, silver and bronze, to cut and set stones, to work in wood, and to engage in all kinds of crafts. Moreover, I have appointed Oholiab son of Ahisamak, of the tribe of Dan, to help him. Also I have given ability to all the skilled workers to make everything I have commanded you." (Exod. 31:1–6, TNIV)

Thank God for Bezalel and Oholiab.

Then there was Nehemiah, who had some men help build the walls, while others were skilled to assist in the fighting. Solomon summoned a man named Huram all the way from Tyre because of his great reputation as the best bronze worker alive. We can't forget about Paul, who was great at making tents, or Jesus, who was a trained carpenter.

Countless numbers of people today have special talents and are being used by God in great ways. There are writers, musicians, teachers, artists, handymen, graphic designers, sheetrock workers, bookkeepers, landscapers, and auto mechanics, just to name a few. All have found a way to use their talents to serve others. How about you? What are you good at? What really interests you? What are some of your hobbies? How are you using your talents to serve others?

---

George Brunstad is a retired American Airlines pilot who also happens to be the uncle of actor Matt Damon. George is the oldest person to ever swim the English Channel. This seventy-year-old Ridgefield, Connecticut, native did it in fifteen hours and fifty-nine minutes early on Sunday morning, August 29, 2004. George emerged from the water on the shores of France after his thirty-two-mile victory swim. Holding up the arms of two supporting swimmers by his side, he gave the *Rocky* salute, exclaiming "Praise the Lord! God is good."

George credited the Lord for the water's good conditions. "God placed His hand on it," he said. Some members of Wilton Baptist Church were with him, and his home congregation prayed for him hour by hour.

Faith and prayer moved him to victory, but there was something else quite poignant in his motivation. George had visited an orphanage with a church group in the poverty-stricken town of Hinche in Haiti's central highlands. He was so impacted that he decided to swim the English Channel to raise awareness of this great need and to raise money to build an orphanage, school, and medical center for Hinche's children. He swam for a higher purpose.

As he crossed the English Channel, his mind was fixed on those children. That's what kept him going, he said. And he raised more than $11,000 for the project. With a vision from God, compassion in his heart, and natural ability, George Brunstad provides an example for Christians, both young and old, of how God can use any talent to fulfill His purposes.[3]

---

## Identifying Your Talents

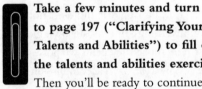 Take a few minutes and turn to page 197 ("Clarifying Your Talents and Abilities") to fill out the talents and abilities exercise. Then you'll be ready to continue reading.

## Developing Your Talents and Abilities

There is an element to your talents that is your responsibility: you are supposed to use them! Jesus made it clear, in the parable of the talents, that those who didn't invest their talents wisely would face great judgment. To the servant who hid his money instead of investing it, the master said, "That's a terrible way to live! It's criminal to live cautiously like that! If you knew I was after the best, why did you do less than the least?" (Matt. 25:26, MSG).

## Understanding Your Talents to Fulfill Your Purpose

Hopefully, the exercises in this book are helping you to better define how God made you and how each of the seven components applies to your purpose. Each one is equally important to fulfilling your God-intended design. Just as a puzzle needs every piece to be complete, so your life needs each piece operating in its place for you to be fully functional. Here are some hints that will help you better understand how to apply your talents to your purpose:

• Use your unique blend of talents, passions, and spiritual gifts to help others.

• Be happy with how God made you. God designed you with unique talents–He needs you to be uniquely you.

• Take time to develop your talents and abilities. Create habits that will develop your talents so that when the opportunities come, you'll be ready.

• Don't rely too heavily on your talents. These were given to you as a means to glorify God–not yourself. Keep your motives pure.

• Find the talents that best fit you. Not all areas of talent may apply to fulfilling your purpose. Find and develop talents you are passionate about applying to ministry.

God has done His part by placing these talents in your life when you were a tiny embryo. Your job now is to define them and develop them.

As defined by Marcus Buckingham, "Talent is any recurring pattern of thought, feeling, or behavior that is productively applied."[5] We must dedicate ourselves to perfecting our talents, creating positive habits so that when the opportunity presents itself, we can master the challenge with excellence.

One of the dangers we face when serving in an area in which we excel is the tendency to rely on our own natural strengths, instead of utterly depending on God. Our talents were given to us as a means of glorifying God, not circumventing Him for our own glory. Just remember, the talents we possess are simply a *means* to accomplish an end, not an end themselves. Our motives and focus must remain pure!

## Finding the Talents That Best Fit You

Maybe you've identified your talents but find that you feel absolutely no passion to use them for any kind of service. Just a few months ago, I was talking with Bill, who is a very gifted computer technician. Quite boldly he said, "The last thing I want to do when I get off work is to come to the church and work some more." There is some merit to his unwillingness to use his talent. It isn't coupled with a passion in that area!

Not all areas of talent will apply to fulfilling your purpose. For Bill, his expertise in computers is not a talent he wishes to pursue anywhere outside of his work environment. However, when I asked Bill what other talents he had that excited him, he quickly responded, "That's easy. I enjoy soccer, and I'd love to work with young kids to teach them how to play the game." There you have it! Turn off your computer talent and start kicking the ball. By the way, one of Bill's spiritual gifts is teaching, and one of his passion expressions is motivating ... and he also enjoys mentoring young people. Bill now uses his talents, passions, and spiritual gifts as a soccer coach for his church's high-school soccer team.

My conversation with Bill reminds me of a statement made by one of our previous Supreme Court justices. When he retired, Justice Thurgood Marshall remarked, "I did what I could with what I had."[5] How about you? Are you doing what you can with all that you have?

# CHAPTER EIGHT

# MIRROR, MIRROR ON THE WALL ...

## MAKING SENSE OF YOUR PERSONAL MAKEUP

"You made all the delicate, inner parts of my
body and knit me together in my mother's womb.
Thank you for making me so wonderfully
complex! Your workmanship is marvelous—
and how well I know it."

—Psalm 139:13–14, NLT

D ear Andy,
I'm thinking of you today, hoping you feel better. You are so
special; everything about you was perfectly designed. In fact, in the
gumball machine of life, I just know you're a green one, because they're
my favorite kind! You know what—I think the Cubs are going to win the
ballgame this weekend! We'll see, I guess. Andy, I'm glad to have you for
a friend. I love you.

—Your Secret Pal

Letters to Andy came mysteriously but predictably. His Secret Pal was consistent and determined to cheer him up. Any other mom would do the same.

Linda Bremner says of her letter-writing stunt, "I began to write him as a
secret pal ... I thought I was doing something really smart." Andy, who suffered from a type of cancer called non-Hodgkin's lymphoma, wasn't fooled.

About a month after his Secret Pal began sending him letters, Andy figured it out. He gave her a drawing to be delivered to his "Secret Pal." When she opened it, it said, "Mom, I love you." Her cover was blown, but the two never mentioned it again, and Andy continued to receive letters from his Secret Pal until August 31, 1984, when his battle with cancer ended. He was almost twelve years old.

"Although I had two other children, the grief and pain of losing Andy was unbearable," Linda says. "I felt my life was over because his was over." She felt purposeless, wondering how she would survive in the midst of sorrow.

Sorting through Andy's personal items after his death, she found a shoebox packed with love letters from his Secret Pal. He had kept every letter. Inside was also an address book with the names of children he had befriended at a camp for kids with cancer. If these kids were special to Andy, they were special to her, too. Linda thought the very least she could do was send them a card to lift their spirits, just like she had done so many times for her own little boy. Besides, she thought, it would help her feel better doing something to cheer them up.

Before long, one of Andy's friends responded, thanking her for the card. "I didn't think anyone knew I lived," he said. These simple words from a little boy, desperate to be wished well or even acknowledged, ignited in her a passion and determination to touch the lives of children who, like Andy, suffered from illness.

And so Love Letters, Inc. was born. Word quickly spread, and requests for letters began piling up. Linda recruited a small army of volunteers, and they started writing letters and making cards. Linda made an appeal for donations of stamps through a nationwide campaign of postmarked love.

Linda Bremner and her compassionate team of volunteers sent more than 1,200 letters, gifts, and cards *every week* to children who were burn victims and accident survivors or who suffered from cancer, muscular dystrophy, AIDS,

After a stop at Starbucks for an extra-hot no-foam venti non-fat vanilla latte (which, of course, will only help you see colors more clearly), you finally arrive at Home Depot. It is easier (or more satisfying) to gather 750 paint chips *one at a time* rather than just grabbing them and sorting them out later. And "since we're already here," you'd better take a look at towel racks, toilets, tile, and trim. Off to twelve more showrooms ...

When you get back home, you check the mail and find the new Pottery Barn catalog. Not a moment too soon! It's a good thing this timeless work of literature arrived so you and your husband can make spontaneous choices for duvet covers, pillows, and shams. After all, how can you paint the room and keep the old, perfectly good bedding that happened to be purchased from last year's catalog?

Once each catalog selection has been cut out and pinned to the wall, paint chips and tiles strewn about the floor, you can stand back and marvel at the day's accomplishments. Then, and only then, can you "budget" the project, scribbling a ballpark estimate on the back of a paint swatch and figuring you can probably have it all done by Thanksgiving.

You get my point. We're different!

---

## The Bible and Personal Makeup

One doesn't have to look very deep into Scripture to realize that God used all kinds of people to further His kingdom.

Peter was known for his brash and impetuous personality. He was the one who "had a sword, drew it and struck the high priest's servant, cutting off his right ear" (John 18:10, TNIV). When Jesus challenged the disciples to step out of the boat onto the water, only Peter "got down out of the boat, walked on the water and came toward Jesus" (Matt. 14:29, TNIV). He was the one who defiantly blurted out to Jesus, "Even if all fall away on account of you, I never will" (Matt. 26:33, TNIV), only to disappoint his Lord and himself with three statements of denial. Peter entered the tomb first (Luke 24:12). It is evident that he was an outgoing, outspoken guy.

Paul, meanwhile, was a ruthless defender of the faith—strategic, determined, and persistent. From his prison cell he confirmed his countenance: "Having become confident by my chains, I am much bolder to speak the word without fear" (Phil. 1:13, TNIV). Paul would never give up! He was also a great thinker and eloquent writer who penned more than two-thirds of the New Testament, each epistle further defining Paul as one of strong feelings and strong convictions. His all-or-nothing approach is demonstrated in the following statement: "What is more, I consider everything a loss because of the surpassing worth of knowing Christ Jesus my Lord, for whose sake I have lost all things. I consider them garbage, that I may gain Christ" (Phil. 3:8, TNIV). Whether he was persecuting the Church or dying for it, his life was one of passion, perseverance, and pursuit.

Then there's Barnabas, the encourager, the peacemaker. Luke calls him "a good man" (Acts 11:24, TNIV). His name actually means "son of encouragement" (Acts 4:36). He loved people immensely, wanted everyone to get along (Acts 15:36–39), and was willing to sell his possessions to help others in need (Acts 4:37). Barnabas was a friend of friends; a real people-person.

Whether you're spontaneous and daring like Peter, determined like Paul, or personable like Barnabas, God will use your personal makeup to accomplish great things.

I have a friend named Lori Simpson who faithfully serves as a volunteer in her church two or three days a week, six to eight hours a day. That's almost twenty-five hours a week and more than 1,000 hours per year … totally free of financial compensation. Now, virtually every department at our church clamors to have Lori help them because she's great at getting stuff done. Her secret is simple: she is who God made her, and that's that. You will never see her on the platform in front of people. She prefers to remain anonymous, simply serving, quietly giving. She understands her personal makeup and is actively fulfilling her purpose.

## What Is Personal Makeup?

There are as many definitions of "personal makeup" as there are opinions on the subject. However, I want to focus on a simplistic, clear, and concise definition as a springboard for the rest of this chapter: your personal makeup is a God-given internal filter that determines how you relate to every person and every situation.

In other words, your personal makeup is the combination of multiple inborn traits that, in partnership with the Holy Spirit, help you fulfill your intended, God-given purpose. Your personal makeup was designed specifically for you by God. It stays with you for your entire life. Although there are many internal and external influences that can affect the way your personal makeup is displayed, it will always be part of who you are.

A person who, by nature, has a tendency to be structured and task-focused will always be that way. His pre-Christ life may be marked by a drive to succeed at any cost, and this does not change even after he comes to the saving knowledge of Jesus Christ and becomes completely new (2 Cor. 5:17). The only difference is that he is now challenged to adjust his character and personality as Christ becomes a predominant influence in his life.

In his Network Resource Kit, Bruce Bugbee developed a very simplistic yet proven assessment tool for identifying the four potential types of personal makeup or "styles."[2] With some minor modifications, we'll focus on using this excellent assessment tool as the primary means to define personal makeup. Your personal makeup will be defined by one of the following four quadrants:

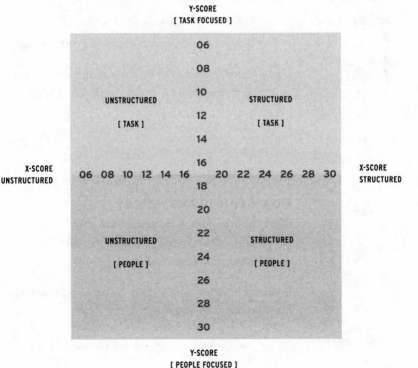

Your personal makeup is determined by how you score on two intersecting axes (X and Y, Structured/Unstructured and Task-Focused/People-Focused, respectively). Later on in this chapter, you will be asked to follow a detailed exercise in Part Four that will better define these axes and how to arrive at your score. Let's look at the following areas to help you better understand what these axes represent.

## How Do You Handle Things? [X Axis]

There are two sides to the first axis, structured and unstructured, as illustrated below. You will fall somewhere between the two extremes.

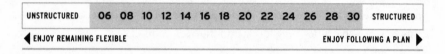

| UNSTRUCTURED | 06 | 08 | 10 | 12 | 14 | 16 | 18 | 20 | 22 | 24 | 26 | 28 | 30 | STRUCTURED |
| --- | --- | --- | --- | --- | --- | --- | --- | --- | --- | --- | --- | --- | --- | --- |
| ◀ ENJOY REMAINING FLEXIBLE | | | | | | | | | | | ENJOY FOLLOWING A PLAN ▶ | | |

If you consider yourself to be more of a structured person, you may consider serving in an area that:

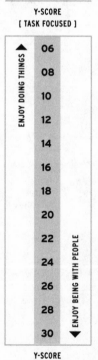

Y-SCORE
[ TASK FOCUSED ]

ENJOY DOING THINGS ▲
06
08
10
12
14
16
18
20
22
24
26
28
30 ▼

ENJOY BEING WITH PEOPLE

Y-SCORE
[ PEOPLE FOCUSED ]

• Focuses on organizing, planning, and administration.

• Follows a set schedule or program.

• May need assistance in organizing or planning.

If you consider yourself to be more of an unstructured person, you may consider serving in an area that allows:

• More flexibility in *how* you serve.

• More flexibility in *when* you serve.

• Many options as to *where* you serve.

## How Are You Motivated? [Y Axis]

There are two sides to the second axis, task-focused and people-focused, as illustrated below. You will fall somewhere between the two extremes.

If you are a person who focuses on tasks, you may consider serving in an area that:

• Focuses your energy toward accomplishing tasks.

• Has specific goals that allow a sense of accomplishment.

• Clearly defines the function and expectation of where you are to serve.

If you focus more on people, you may consider serving in an area that:

• Allows you the ability to interact with people regularly.

• Is built on establishing relationships and helping people.

• Gives you the time to meet the needs of others.

## Defining Your Personal Makeup

In the previous three chapters, you were asked to pause for a self-discovery exercise. These exercises are designed to help you understand how God made you and how each area applies to your fulfilled destiny. This personal makeup exercise is the fourth of seven self-discovery tools. **Turn to page 201 ("Learning About Your Personal Makeup") and complete the exercise.** Once you are finished, return to this page and read the rest of the chapter.

## Benefits of Serving in Your Personal Makeup Strengths

Identifying your personal makeup and learning how it affects every aspect of your life can be liberating. Many today live with frustration and disappointment simply because they don't understand how God fashioned them. Here are a few benefits to consider as you move forward in discovering your personal makeup.

**You will find fulfillment if you accept who God made you to be.** Unfortunately, many spend their entire lives trying to be like someone else, only to live a life of emptiness and

### Understanding Your Personal Makeup Assessment Results

Take a moment and consider your results. Do they surprise you? Do your results help you define why you excel in some areas, yet struggle in others? Are there some relational differences that suddenly seem to make more sense? Do you see how these results could further clarify areas in which you would want to serve? Hopefully, this simple tool has helped you further understand how God made you.

This is by no means an exhaustive behavioral study. It is simply a tool that helps each person better understand his or her unique personal makeup and how it might affect his or her purpose. Here are some things to consider about your results:

### Varying Degrees of Scoring on the Axis Lines

Those who scored further from the center may want to consider pursuing an area to serve that is best described by their quadrant. Those who are closer to the center may have more of a natural tendency to serve in a secondary, adjoining quadrant.

### Scoring on a Line

Those who scored on or close to either axis may find themselves able to serve in either of the two adjoining quadrants.

### Flexibility in an Area of Service

Regardless of where you scored in this assessment, you still have the flexibility to serve in another area and serve well.

### Using Passions, Spiritual Gifts, Talents, and Personal Makeup Together

Your personal makeup was designed to complement the other six components that make you uniquely you. Understanding how these components work together will bring great joy and fulfillment in serving as you find the place where you thrive.

despair. What you believe about yourself and who you're supposed to be will have a much greater impact on your life than what any other person believes.

**You will better enjoy the area where you serve.**
Rick Warren says, "It feels good to do what God made you to do."[3] He goes on to explain that God never intended for you to experience anxiety in serving. Rather, He wants you to experience joy and be full of glory.

**You will be more fruitful in serving in an area that best fits who you are.**
When you're placed in an environment that brings tension and anxiety, your ability to excel is greatly diminished. On the other hand, finding the right place to serve that matches your personal makeup may allow you to touch thousands of lives!

**You will have a better appreciation for others who serve with you.**
When each person understands his or her role, things just seem to gel more easily. Knowing that you are where God wants you helps to prevent competition and jealousy from creeping in.

## Other Considerations Regarding Your Personal Makeup

Focusing on your personal makeup can be as much a blessing as a curse. Prayerfully consider these six cautions.

**Every type of personal makeup and its degrees of intensity are equal in value.**

Every person has been intentionally designed by the Creator of the universe to be exactly who he or she is. God didn't make mistakes when He carefully knit us together. Your personal makeup is deliberate. Don't view it as inferior or superior to the makeup of those around you.

**Don't overemphasize or underestimate your personal makeup. Find a balance.**

Your personal makeup is only one of many components God intended to assist in fulfilling your purpose. The recognition of specific traits isn't a license to dominate situations or crawl into a hole and wait for Jesus' return. Let the Holy Spirit direct you toward the perfect balance in maximizing your personal makeup.

**Don't confuse your personal makeup with your character.**

Your personal makeup is the combination of inborn traits you use in partnership with the Holy Spirit to fulfill your intended purpose. Character is the one thing we develop in this world and take with us into the next. We must never confuse the two! Your personal makeup can have either a positive or negative effect on your life and on the lives of those around you. Your character is the rudder that determines the course.

**Don't use your personal makeup as an excuse not to address character issues.**

It's easy to use personal makeup as an excuse not to change areas in your life that may appear to have character flaws. Have you ever heard someone say, "I can't help it; that's just the way I am"? That may be his or her opinion, but it definitely isn't reality or God's will.

**Don't use your personal makeup as an excuse not to serve when asked.**

Each of us should be willing to help anyone at any time. God measures success not necessarily by what we gain but by what we give away, including our time and energy. Serving with the right motive for the right purpose, regardless of your personal makeup, releases God's favor and blessing on our lives. We must willingly give up our own rights and interests for the sake of others.

**Learn to appreciate others' personal makeup in working environments.**

John Ortberg's book *Everybody's Normal Till You Get to Know Them* is an excellent book on this topic. Learning to appreciate everyone's differences is a great skill to master. When we learn to *understand* before developing the expectation of being *understood*, we create an environment where everyone can succeed.

> **WHEN WE LEARN TO UNDERSTAND BEFORE DEVELOPING THE EXPECTATION OF BEING UNDERSTOOD, WE CREATE AN ENVIRONMENT WHERE EVERYONE CAN SUCCEED.**

There is great power in learning to embrace the different angles from which others may approach situations. Different perspectives can offer a well-rounded solution instead of your one-dimensional approach. Your way may not be the best way or even the right way, but only a *different* way. Learn to accept and appreciate others' personal makeup in any working environment.

Thank God for His diversity. The world is teeming with all types of people, each created with specific callings and purposes. He has fashioned us with unique passions, supernatural gifts, and a complete set of natural abilities. Our personal makeup is layered over the top of each of these, giving every person a very unique place on God's team.

# CHAPTER NINE

# HURTS SO GOOD
## USING LIFE EXPERIENCES TO YOUR BENEFIT

> "Every detail works to your advantage and to
> God's glory: more and more grace, more and more
> people, more and more praise! So we're not giving
> up. How could we! Even though on the outside it
> often looks like things are falling apart on us, on
> the inside, where God is making new life, not a day
> goes by without his unfolding grace. These hard
> times are small potatoes compared to the coming
> good times, the lavish celebration prepared for us.
> There's far more here than meets the eye."
>
> —2 Corinthians 4:15–18, MSG

L ife. For most of us, it's a sequence of fickle paths filled with twists and spirals—a succession of events fair and unfair, tragic and comic, spellbinding and lackluster. The way it begins, the way it ends, and what we do with it in between (not to mention what everything in between does to *us*) becomes the story of our lives. So it was with Zarah Dupree.

Zarah grew up in the sleepy farm town of Woodland, California. The youngest of three children, she was the only girl.

Zarah's father was a highly decorated Army sergeant who fought in Germany during World War II at the Battle of the Bulge. He became a sheriff after the war and later worked as a private investigator. "I remember my father always had a gun, either in a shoulder holster under his left arm or under the seat of the car. He always told great stories about his combat experiences in the war. He was very proud to serve his country."

But Zarah could tell early on that the war had taken something from him that he never fully regained. He was numb emotionally. He eventually left as Zarah's parents divorced and never came back.

"I wish he could've been there for me during my difficult years," she says. "Little did I know the impact his absence would have later on." Zarah spent her adolescent years confused and searching, wondering who she was, who she was supposed to be, what she was supposed to do.

She was sexually abused by two family members after her parents' divorce, and she began to withdraw into books, writing, and music. "I realize now that I was confused about my gender because I had always identified with my father, who was strong and who could do anything he wanted. I didn't identify with my mother, because she seemed weak by comparison and emotionally distant [since] she was trying to keep the family together and didn't have time to nurture me during the years I was forming my female identity."

Zarah came out of the closet at age nineteen. She had a series of failed relationships over the next twenty-five years, including a lesbian "marriage" for more than six years. "Eventually it ended in a very ugly way," Zarah says. "I was really disillusioned by the whole homosexual life I had built for myself, and I was searching. I had been involved in gay organizations, and I was a visible figure in gay and lesbian twelve-step recovery programs and other causes, yet I was feeling in my heart that God wanted more *for* me and *from* me than this."

Throughout much of her adult life, Zarah's experiences always led her back to the memory of one night when she had first suspected that somehow, God had His hand on her, protecting her and keeping her safe.

"One evening, I was lying in my bed waiting to fall asleep when this great golden light engulfed my bedroom and surrounded me with this sparkling electric energy. At the time, I remember thinking it was my guardian angel. I always felt protected on some level after that … I felt different and that I was somehow special in God's eyes. It wasn't the kind of "special" that makes you more important than others, but the knowledge that no matter how unimportant I felt, I'd always be important to God. I believe God wanted me to know that early on because of what I was to go through later on."

During the early years of her life, Zarah had five near-death experiences. She was born a "blue baby" and received a blood transfusion as a newborn. In 1955, this was a new and risky procedure, but it spared her life. As a small child, she almost drowned at the bottom of a pool. Over the years, she survived eight different car accidents, breaking thirty-six bones and enduring twenty-one surgeries. On two separate occasions, Zarah actually died on the operating table and was narrowly revived by surgeons.

Obviously, her childhood inkling was correct ... she was special in God's eyes; He had spared her time and again for an important purpose. But what?

One day, after a divine set of circumstances, Zarah found herself walking through the front doors of the Brooklyn Tabernacle in New York City, where she would surrender her life to Jesus Christ—a new start, a new life, a new future!

Today, through her local church, Zarah leads a successful small group that reaches out to people who struggle with homosexuality and same-sex attraction. She has also set her sights on relatives and friends of those trapped in the homosexual lifestyle, helping them understand why the bondages of homosexuality have such a tight grip, and showing the way of escape found through Calvary.

"The Lord wants me to shout from the mountaintops that life really matters! After everything that's happened in my life, I know that what I have is the most blessed life on earth. One of my favorite Scriptures is 'My grace is sufficient for you' (2 Cor. 12:9). If I can help just one other person understand what that means, my life would count for something, and it doesn't matter if anyone else knows about it. God knows, and that's what truly matters."[1]

---

## What Good Are Life Experiences, Anyway?

There is purpose to our lives, greater purpose than happiness alone. Throughout our lifetime, God will allow or divinely place circumstances along our journey that will put us face to face with certain issues we are to resolve. How we respond to these trials is of the utmost importance. Charles Swindoll says, "I am convinced that life is 10 percent what happens to me and 90 percent how I react to it."[2]

The Bible substantiates this point in 1 Peter 4:12–13: "Friends, when life gets really difficult, don't jump to the conclusion that God isn't on the job. Instead, be glad that you are in the very thick of what Christ experienced. This is a spiritual refining process, with glory just around the corner" (MSG).

Not all life experiences are meant to be bad. There are times (hopefully many) when God allows us to experience His goodness through His favor and blessings. Maybe you were mentored by a great man or woman of God, and that experience played a role in shaping you. Or you might have attended a great college or university, and that experience helped define who you are today. Maybe you were raised in a wonderful family environment, with a solid foundation of biblical morals and values. These are some of life's most positive experiences. The bottom line is that God intends to use every life experience, whether good or bad, to shape you into a person who is fully able and prepared to fulfill your purpose. Over the years, I've developed a working definition of life experiences: certain events or seasons that God allows so you can acquire knowledge, character, and understanding, which can be used to benefit you and others in future situations and ministry opportunities.

> **"I AM CONVINCED THAT LIFE IS 10 PERCENT WHAT HAPPENS TO ME AND 90 PERCENT HOW I REACT TO IT."**
> **–CHARLES SWINDOLL**

Day after day, we will face trials, tragedies, and triumphs that we can't control. We can allow these circumstances to bury us or choose to step up and shake them off. The choice is ours.

These life experiences are only a part of our entire design and are intended to be the refining and strengthening agent of our other components. The previous four chapters have defined the four major components that are placed in our lives by our Creator. Passions, spiritual gifts, talent and abilities, and personal makeup are woven into the fabric of our lives. Life experiences are different in the sense that they are external factors placed in our lives by God to refine us. This refining process works to develop godly character as well as to place us in certain experiences that further shape us into a God-shaped vessel, perfectly crafted for our purpose. After a while, we begin to see that *easy* isn't necessarily synonymous with *good*, and *difficult* isn't necessarily synonymous with *bad*. Sometimes the tough experiences have the greatest refining effect in our lives.

## Types of Life Experiences

Both good experiences and unpleasant ones pop up in every area of our lives. When we understand who we are and where we're going, we have better appreciation of the shaping potential of our life experiences. Zarah Dupree would probably never ask to reenter the painful and destructive lifestyle of her past, but she has learned to appreciate how those experiences have equipped her to fulfill her purpose. Her ability to reach successfully into the dark lives of those bound by homosexuality has come from her real-life experiences. The apostle Paul eloquently confirmed this process in his address to the Corinthians: "He comes alongside us when we go through hard times, and before you know it, he brings us alongside someone else who is going through hard times so that we can be there for that person just as God was there for us" (2 Cor. 1:4, MSG).

Life experiences come from a myriad of sources. They include (but are not limited to) the following:

### Your Family Background

Stop for a moment and consider your family background. What kind of environment were you raised in? What religious beliefs surrounded you? What country and culture did your family live in? The answers to each of these questions may have an impact on your purpose and how God has shaped you.

I was raised in a home where my father didn't believe in God. My mother was raised as a Catholic, but religion wasn't part of our upbringing. My only memory of attending any church service was going to a Christian Science church once and a Mormon church with some friends, and that's it. When I gave my life to Christ, I immediately found a passion for reaching the lost. I spent hours studying different religions and belief systems, hoping that I might reach those who need Christ, and this is still a driving passion in my life today. Looking back, I believe my upbringing had great influence on my desire to reach lost people.

### Your Health

Hopefully, most of you have lived a relatively healthy life. But why have

some people been born with life-altering diseases and deformities? Why
do some face tragic accidents or crippling diseases and become maimed or
impaired for life? Those are questions only God can answer. King Solomon
concluded, "Whatever God does, that's the way it's going to be, always. No
addition, no subtraction. God's done it and that's it. That's so we'll quit asking
questions and simply worship in holy fear. Whatever was, is. Whatever will
be, is. That's how it always is with God" (Eccles. 3:14–15, MSG).

Although we might never know the answers to these questions, we definitely
know that God has made clear what we are supposed to do about these issues:
use them for His purposes. I am quickly reminded of many incredible people
who have faced trials and used them to impact history. Helen Keller, born
blind and deaf, chose to overcome her life experiences and challenge even the
healthiest of people to live deliberate lives of purpose. Joni Eareckson Tada,
crippled from the neck down in a diving accident, uses her life experience to
show the world that you can overcome the greatest of tragedies and allows it
to be a testimony of God's glory.

**Your Finances**
What is the current state of your finances? How has God challenged you
regarding them? Could it be that He has allowed certain financial successes or
tragedies in your life as part of your perfect design in fulfilling your purpose?

God has a way of using our financial world to both shape our lives and build
His kingdom. I love the way Eugene Peterson translates the words of Jesus:
"Don't hoard treasure down here where it gets eaten by moths and cor-
roded by rust or—worse!—stolen by burglars. Stockpile treasure in heaven,
where it's safe from moth and rust and burglars. It's obvious, isn't it? The
place where your treasure is, is the place you will most want to be, and end
up being" (Matt. 6:19–21, MSG). Clearly, finances have a profound way of
affecting our lives.

Remember Millard Fuller, founder of Habitat for Humanity? God used
finances to both get his attention and redirect his life. In the process, finances
helped him fulfill his purpose of touching thousands of people in need of
housing. Millard understands financial life experiences!

A nother person who has taken his financial life experiences seriously is the founder and current CEO of Chick-fil-A, S. Truett Cathy. His biblical perspective on both life and business has allowed him to build the second-largest quick-service chicken restaurant chain in the United States. Since Chick-fil-A's inception in 1967, S. Truett Cathy has held to the biblical conviction that what we have is meant to bless others. "Nearly every moment of every day we have the opportunity to give something to someone else—our time, our love, our resources," he said. "I have always found more joy in giving when I did not expect anything in return." He has backed this statement by giving more than $20 million to charities, and some reports claim he gives up to 90 percent of his personal income back to God.[3]

**Your Vocation**

Have you ever wondered why you were hired by a certain company or why you serve in the position you do? Have you ever paused and looked back at all of your work experience and noticed some common thread woven through it all? It could be that your vocational experiences have been placed in your life to give you the experience or platform you need to fulfill your purpose.

**Your Ministry**

Don't let the word *ministry* throw you off course, as if it doesn't apply to you. Ministry can be defined simply as the place where you invest your time, energy, and resources to advance God's kingdom. You don't have to be on staff at a local church to be in ministry. Every believer, regardless of occupational status, should have a place to minister through his or her local church.

You may have already found great joy serving in some form of ministry. You may still be on your journey toward deciphering where you fit into God's plan. Whether you have served in numerous ministry positions or just started your very first assignment, these ministry situations will be a big part of shaping your life.

Where are you currently serving? Have you considered what valuable lessons you are learning? Maybe it is character issues. You might be learning some new skills. There might be someone who is speaking into your life. Whatever the case may be, your ministry experiences will play a great role in giving you the tools needed to live life on purpose.

## Your Education

Your education plays an important role in shaping who you are. Depending on the focus and intensity, education can go as far as shaping your religious beliefs and worldview. Regardless of your educational background, every academic area can be used in fulfilling your purpose. You bring to the table expertise in an area that may be lacking in your local church. Even Paul used his great knowledge of the law as a foundation for writing his large repertoire of the epistles. Maybe it's time that you stepped up and used your educational experiences to make your life count?

> "EVERYTHING HAPPENING TO ME IN THIS JAIL ONLY SERVES TO MAKE CHRIST MORE ACCURATELY KNOWN, REGARDLESS OF WHETHER I LIVE OR DIE. THEY DIDN'T SHUT ME UP; THEY GAVE ME A PULPIT! ALIVE, I'M CHRIST'S MESSENGER; DEAD, I'M HIS BOUNTY. LIFE VERSUS EVEN MORE LIFE! I CAN'T LOSE."
> —PHILIPPIANS 1:20-21, MSG

## Life Challenges

Some of the most difficult yet most fruitful life experiences are found in the trials and tribulations we face while simply living life.

Paul understood these challenges and wrote about finding the ability to turn tragedy into triumph. On one occasion while being imprisoned, he wrote, "Everything happening to me in this jail only serves to make Christ more accurately known, regardless of whether I live or die. They didn't shut me up; they gave me a pulpit! Alive, I'm Christ's messenger; dead, I'm his bounty. Life versus even more life! I can't lose" (Phil. 1:20–21, MSG). With God on our side, we will never lose; if He is for us, who can be against us?

Life challenges come in many forms—illness, loss of a spouse or child, devastating fires or floods, divorce … the list goes on. With a proper heart and attitude, God can use any challenge in life—regardless of the circumstance—to further you along toward your purpose. There might be addictions or past sins that have plagued you. I have seen many who have struggled for years with pornography and then have been delivered, who turn around and use that ugly experience as a means to rescue others struggling with the same sin. The death of a loved one may have literally paralyzed your life, causing such great depression that you can barely even function, much less minister to others. However, even this tragedy can be used in building ministries to reach out to those in seasons of grief. Although God might not be the one who initiates these life challenges, He intends to use each of them as a means to fulfill His purpose in our lives.

## What Are Your Life Experiences?

You've probably reflected on some of your own personal life experiences while reading these last few pages. Woven into our memory is a lifetime of experiences that have helped shape us into who we are. **Please turn to the self-discovery exercise in Part Four on page 203 ("Making Sense of Your Life Experiences").** This exercise will shed new light on your life and how each of these experiences can be used toward fulfilling your purpose. Once you've answered the questions, you'll be ready to finish reading the rest of this chapter.

## Life Experiences Are to Help You, Not Hurt You

The Old Testament is filled with examples of how God used life experiences in forming the destiny of those He loved. Most notable are the children of Israel and their journey from bondage in Egypt (which represents life before Christ), through the Red Sea (conversion experience), into the wilderness (life as a Christian), and the Promised Land (the promise of eternity in heaven). Keep in mind, the end goal was not happiness in the wilderness, but reaching their destination. Here, in this framework, Moses wrote, "Remember every road that God led you on for those forty years in the wilderness, pushing you to your limits, testing you so that he would know what you were made of, whether you would keep his commandments or not. He put you through hard times. He made you go hungry" (Deut. 8:2–3, MSG). Sound pretty compassionate? Loving? Well, let the guy finish. "Your clothes didn't wear out and your feet didn't blister those forty years. You learned deep in your heart that God disciplines you in the same ways a father disciplines his child" (Deut. 8:4–5, MSG).

The point is this: the trials that God allows you to face are His way of lovingly disciplining you to ultimately help you reach your destination. He is dedicated to helping you, not hurting you, even if it means placing obstacles in your life to get your attention.

We've been given the all-encompassing task of finding out what opportunities are awaiting us beyond our own life experiences. Though life's bruises might have hurt, their outcome is destined for our good. Here are a few things the Bible promises. Life experiences will:

- Make you more like Jesus (1 Pet. 4:12–13).
- Give you compassion to minister to others (2 Cor. 1:4).
- Draw you closer to Jesus (Ps. 34:18).
- Create a greater dependence on God (2 Cor. 1:9).
- Make you a stronger person (Rom. 5:3–4).
- Allow you the opportunity to participate in God's riches (Rom. 8:17).
- Are tools used in fulfilling your purpose (Gen. 50:20).
- Promise you a better life (Heb. 12:11).
- Give you a better perspective on life (Deut. 8:4–5).
- Make you more humble (Heb. 12:10).
- Achieve eternal glory (2 Cor. 4:17).

How refreshing to know that God has taken great interest in our lives! We haven't been left alone, and He has set us on a course to accomplish great things during our lifetime. He guides us, directs us, disciplines us, challenges us … all because He loves us. Our responsibility is to set our sights on our purpose, to not lose heart, and to never give up.

CHAPTER TEN

# IT'S TIME TO GROW UP

## GROWING UP AND USING YOUR
## SPIRITUAL MATURITY

> "I ask—ask the God of our Master, Jesus Christ,
> the God of glory—to make you intelligent and
> discerning in knowing him personally, your eyes
> focused and clear, so that you can see exactly what
> it is he is calling you to do, grasp the immensity of
> this glorious way of life he has for Christians, oh,
> the utter extravagance of his work in us who trust
> him—endless energy, boundless strength!"
>
> —Ephesians 1:17–19, MSG

From his earliest recollection, Dick Iverson can remember always having the desire to devote himself to the purposes of God. It started in a tent revival at age eight. "The evangelist was speaking on hell and said all thieves and liars were going to hell," he says. "I fell under immediate conviction because I had just stolen some cookies and then lied to my parents about it. This double crime sent me down the sawdust aisle where I would have a life-changing experience. Christ would come into my life, and I would devote the rest of my life to His cause."

It was evident through his childhood and adolescent years that Dick had built a lifestyle of serving God. Growing in spiritual health and maturity seemed only logical if he were to fulfill the dreams God placed in his heart. "Even at the age of eleven, I remember having a deep hunger for God. I wanted more of Him, which caused me to pursue Him every chance that I could." This passion to serve God and conviction to never be a casual Christian galvanized his pursuit of growing in God every day, at every moment with every decision.

When his family moved to Portland when Dick was thirteen, he began to be influenced and mentored by a nineteen-year-old preacher named Tommy L. Osborn (now known as one of the greatest evangelists of his time).

"Pastor Osborn made quite an impact on my life and helped me to really appreciate the Word of God and His powerful presence. I can remember in one of his meetings the Lord spoke to me and said, 'I have put My hand on you for the ministry.'"

But Dick understood that this revelation was his *potential* future. He knew he had a part to play: to fully dedicate himself to God's purposes and live a life of discipline and growth. He knew that his destiny was directly dependent upon his spiritual health, growth, and maturity. Somehow he knew character preceded gifting, and his level of maturity determined the outcome of that.

"Right after my high-school graduation, I received a letter from T. L. Osborn inviting me to come and join his evangelistic team to watch over the big tent they were using for revival meetings. Coming into a tent with more than eight thousand people and seeing lives touched by the power of God continued to fuel my passion for ministry." For more than six months Dick was faithful to serve T. L. Osborn, watching, observing, dreaming … believing.

Not long after serving on the T. L. Osborn team, Dick headed off to Jamaica at the age of nineteen to hold his first healing crusade, all on his own. "It started in an unusual way. I received a call from a crusade overseer, who said the preacher was unable to make it and was wondering if I would speak. I was terrified, but still quickly accepted the invitation and headed off to the edge of a small Jamaican town with a large piece of cardboard and pen to post my first crusade sign, 'Evangelist K. R. Iverson, Healing Revival Tonight.' Twelve people showed up for the first Sunday service. I gave it everything I had, and I preached for over an hour. I told everyone the following night we would pray for the sick, and much to my surprise I showed up the second night to a full building and the wonderful presence of God who would begin to heal people right before our eyes."

A nineteen-year-old evangelist holding a packed-out healing crusade in a foreign nation, Dick was beginning to see the fruit of his decision to give God all he had, and this great anointing continued to follow him from his teen years straight through his twenties. Over the next ten years, he traveled as a healing evangelist, mostly overseas, Ireland in particular. Thousands of lives were touched and many were healed. As Dick continued to dedicate himself daily to God's purpose, God continued to honor his pursuit. Although he was off to a great start on his journey to a lifetime of ministry, Dick knew there was much more. He understood that success and fruitfulness isn't measured by how well you start your life and what you accomplish, but by how you finish it.

As Dick began to spiritually mature and his ministry gained velocity, his father, who was the pastor of a small church back in Portland, began to decline in health, and Dick came home to help with the preaching. Over a period of time Dick became the pastor of this very small church and, over the next forty-some years, built one of the most influential churches on the West Coast. "As I look back at those days, I realize that we were coming to a place where God was going to take that little church and make it a flagship to the world." Dick's part was to remain faithful and persistent. God's part was to do the rest.

During his time as senior pastor of Bible Temple (now City Bible Church, led by Pastor Frank Damazio), God used him in incomparable ways. In 1970 Dick launched Portland Bible College, training thousands of students from all over the globe, many who have become great pastors and leaders themselves. In the early 1980s the ministry unveiled City Christian Publishing, which has since distributed millions of books worldwide. As a result of Dick Iverson's ministry, more than fifty churches have been planted and missionaries sent to the far reaches of the globe. He introduced Minister's Fellowship International, which brings together hundreds of pastors and leaders from America, Canada, Africa, Australia, and Europe. Through his willingness to remain faithful and consistent, Dick has found his purpose and is living the life he was supposed to live!

When asked about what he has learned along the way, Dick smiles and replies, "I have to say that I didn't strategize or plan a thing ... I followed the cloud. Sometimes it seemed like nighttime and we had difficult times, but there was always the pillar of fire ... sometimes it was daytime and there was the pillar of smoke. But God has always shown up! I've found that God's plans are always better than my best strategy." And even at seventy-five years old, he is pressing onward, traveling the globe, making the most of every moment, looking forward to every opportunity to grow.[1]

## You Are Destined to Grow

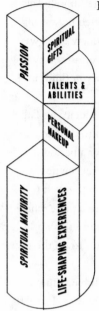

Everything that God has ever created was destined for growth—physical growth, that is. But you and I, we're different than the rest of creation. We are created to grow both physically and spiritually. It's a vibrant, full, and abundant miracle growth. Jesus Himself said, "I came so they can have real and eternal life, more and better life than they ever dreamed of" (John 10:10, MSG). There is no earthly substance that can enhance our growth … all we need is a hunger for what God has for us. In fact, the absence of such amendments doesn't make our spiritual growth any less miraculous, but rather more so. Our blueprint for spiritual growth is as alive as our blueprint for physical growth in our DNA, but we have to feed our spirit properly. Yes, God wants us to have healthy, growing natural bodies, but more importantly, He's passionate about us growing our spiritual man or woman. God wants each of us to make spiritual growth, health, and maturity one of the highest priorities in our life.

How sad it is to see Christians darkening the doorways of their churches every week, only to walk away an hour later unchanged and unchallenged. God isn't interested in how long you've been a Christian or how many services you've attended. Rather, He's concerned with how you have *grown* as a Christian. I have seen young, new converts who are further along on their spiritual path than those who have been Christians for decades. It's a matter of priorities.

## Taking the Pulse of the Church

William Booth, the founder of the Salvation Army, prophesied about the generation of Christians that would enter the twenty-first century: "Six things will dominate this generation; they will have religion without the Holy Spirit, forgiveness without repentance, conversion without new birth, Christianity without Christ, politics without God, and heaven without hell."[2] Sadly enough, his prediction isn't far from the truth.

Christian statistician George Barna confirms the unfortunate fulfillment of this prophecy, revealing some startling statistics about the overall spiritual health of

Christians in America. These indicate that there is not only room for improvement, but also a mandate to prove Booth wrong:

- 95 percent have never led someone to Christ.
- 71 percent of Christians indicate being involved in a local church is their top priority (which means 29 percent don't).
- 40 percent don't believe the Bible to be infallible.
- 35 percent say that bending the rules to get by is all right.
- 26 percent say it doesn't matter which faith you follow; they all teach the same lessons.
- 33 percent believe that abortion is morally acceptable.
- 16 percent are involved of some form of a discipleship group or class at their local church.[3]

Pollster George Gallup confirms these sad truths and is concerned about the maturity of American Christians. Although some 53 percent of the general public say religion is "very important," Gallup found only 13 percent live the faith they profess. He said, "There is not a spiritual vacuum in our country, but spiritual chaos." According to his research, "Americans need instruction badly in Bible study, prayer techniques, and how to share the Gospel. People are trying to be Christian without the Bible." Gallup is a Christian who thinks Americans need more spiritual maturity because they've become consumer-oriented and are practicing what he calls "religion á la carte." He noted, "People want the fruits of faith but not the obligations."[4] Spiritually speaking, we need to grow up!

Are you looking for ways to increase your spiritual health and maturity? Is there a hunger for God's Word and an application of that Word to your life on a daily basis? What about your prayer life? When was the last time you really connected with God? How about your willingness to give consistently and enthusiastically? We are faced every day with the challenge to grow … the choice is ours. If we are going to fulfill our purpose, we've got to grow.

## What Do You Want to Be When You Grow Up?
Throughout the last nine chapters we have discussed God's purpose for your life. There is a definite reason you are here. God has fashioned and formed you with very specific traits. We must make growing in spiritual health and

maturity one of our main priorities in life. Your level of maturity will have a great impact on your level of fruitfulness. God has great plans for you, even beyond your wildest imaginations (Eph. 3:20), and He is simply waiting for you to respond.

Do you know that God is more concerned about *who you are* than *what you do*? It is important that we don't lose sight of the fact that God is more interested in our *motives* for serving than in the actual serving itself. Don't get me wrong: we were created to serve, and we have a purpose to serve. But part of that purpose is to become more like Christ. That's why we are called Christians. Only in our pursuit of becoming more like Him will God allow us to accomplish great things like Him.

The Bible gives us some spiritual ingredients that should be part of the fabric of every believer's life. Obviously each of these components will be at a different level of maturity in each person's life, but our aim should be to master them all and make them part of who we are. In his book, *Vision Management*, Frank Damazio lists twelve spiritual ingredients that make up a mature believer:

- A person who submits to the Lord (Luke 9:23–25, 14:25–35).
- A person who is filled with—and living by—the Holy Spirit (Eph. 5:17–18).
- A person who functions in their spiritual gifts (Rom. 12:1–8).
- A person who commits to and supports the local church (Acts 2:37–47).
- A person who worships fervently (Col. 3:16).
- A person who prays faithfully (Luke 18:1–8).
- A person who consistently shares their faith (1 Pet. 3:15).
- A person who gives generously of their time and resources (2 Cor. 8–9).
- A person who is a family builder (Matt. 19:4–6).
- A person who serves others (Matt. 20:26).
- A person who is overcoming their self-life (Matt. 10:39).
- A person who supports world vision (Matt. 28:20).[5]

This list might be overwhelming to some, but it is by no means an unreachable goal. The Bible says, "I can do all things through Him who strengthens me" (Phil. 4:13, NASB). Even Jesus' own disciples faced the same over-whelming emotions. During His debate with the rich young ruler, Jesus chal-lenged this young man, consumed with the world's pleasures and on a path of growing in the wrong things, to leave it all behind and follow Him. His disciples stood by listening intently. I can just hear their whispers: "Did He say *all?*" "Yep, He said *all.*"

This man who desired God but also desired the world's pleasures left saddened and empty. I'm sure that some of the disciples felt a little overwhelmed at the thought of giving up *everything.* "The disciples were staggered. 'Then who has any chance at all?'" (Matt. 19:25, MSG). Can you relate to this bewildered group of men?

Jesus, seeing their countenance, wood them with some edifying words that were intended to encourage us all: "No chance at all if you think you can pull it off yourself. Every chance in the world if you trust God to do it" (Matt. 19:26, MSG). We don't have to struggle to become all that God wants us to be. He holds the world in the palm of His hand, and He also holds you through every step of your growth process.

## Key Areas of Growth

My wife and I love to work in our yard. It may sound a little strange to you, but the thought of getting lost in a jungle of weeds and dirt brings great rest to my soul. I could relax there for hours, not having to take a single phone call or deal with any crises, chatting with my wife about family, dreams, and goals.

The other day, my wife brought me some great news. A friend of ours had dug up three small cedar trees and said we could have them ... for free. Terrific!

While the trees were free, planting them just about cost me my sanity. This "simple little project" grew in urgency and energy by the moment. Keep in mind these trees were already pulled up, leaving their roots dangerously exposed. So off we went, racing to our friend's home to save these poor little trees before they wilted and died. And because they were small trees and time was of the essence, we rationalized that we should take my Audi sedan; it would get us there in a jiffy and the spacious trunk should be sufficient to keep them comfortable, right?

Wrong. When we arrived, these three "small" trees were more like tower-ing timbers, but I wasn't worried—I'd just leave the trunk open. Being the faithful husband that I am, who loves to work in the garden and please my wife, I loaded these eight-foot evergreens into my three-foot trunk, and off we went like an ambulance screaming down the highway, trying to save the lives of these trees. You should have seen the look on my neighbor's face as we zoomed down our street with these monsters hanging out of the trunk, dragging on the ground. We looked like the Clampetts!

Now, getting home was the easy part. These trees needed to be planted, and fast! Fortunately, we had the perfect spot: alongside our patio to provide a bit more privacy. Unfortunately, that happened to be the rockiest and hardest soil this side of the Ho Chi Minh Trail. And yes, the hole for these "little trees" needed to be four times the size of the root ball (have you ever seen a cedar tree root ball?).

Thank God my wife was there with me, giving me the support I needed to jackhammer through the bottomless pit of rock and solid clay. What I really wanted to do was put those glorified toothpicks in a pile, douse them with jet fuel, and send a plume of black smoke far enough into the sky that my friends six miles away might be able to see the result of their generous gift.

We dug ... and dug ... and dug. And a few hours and four Advils later, we dropped those trees into their new homes. To this day (I'm still crossing my fingers) those trees stand majestically in their new home away from home.

Sounds like a big project, huh? It certainly was. But in a similar way, growing your own spiritual life can be an equally challenging chore. Each of us has been uprooted from the world and given a new place to grow. There's an urgency to protect your new spiritual roots and transplant them into a thriving local church, where you'll have room to grow. The Holy Spirit has does His part, but we must roll up our sleeves and dig and chisel and pound through the hardened chunks of our lives so we have enough room and nourishment to grow. Let's look at three areas you need to tend in order for your spiritual life to mature:

## Christian Foundations

In order for any plant to grow, basic ingredients are needed from the very beginning: water, sun, soil, and nutrients. In the same way, these basic foundations must be present for a Christian to grow into a thriving, mature believer:

• Born again (John 3:3, 16).

• Baptized in water (Acts 2:38–39; Rom. 6:3–5).

• Filled with the Holy Spirit (Mark 16:17–18; Acts 2:4, 10:44–46).

• Planted in a local church (Matt. 16:18, 18:15–20; Heb. 10:24–25).

## Spiritual Disciplines

These foundations will only grow if you are willing to take care of them.
There are some important disciplines that you must apply to your spiritual life
if you want to grow in spiritual health and maturity:

• Reading your Bible regularly (Col. 2:7; 1 Tim. 4:16; 2 Tim. 3:16–17).

• Spending regular times in prayer (Ps. 5:1–3; Jer. 29:12–14).

• Attending church services weekly (Acts 2:1; 1 Cor. 5:4; Heb. 10:24–25).

• Serving in an area of ministry (Matt. 20:28; Rom. 12; Eph. 4:15–16).

• Belonging to a small group-community (Acts 2:42–47, 20:20).

• Faithful giving tithes and offerings (Gen. 14:18–20; Matt. 23:23;
    Heb. 7:1–21).

• Sharing your faith with spiritual seekers (Matt. 28:18–20; 1 Pet. 3:15).

• Discipling others to grow in Christ (Gen. 22:17; Eph. 4:11–13;
    2 Tim. 2:2).

## Christian Character

Your life as a believer should be devoted to serving others and not yourself.
True maturity is measured by how much you build up others rather than
yourself. These principles willingly operating in your life define character and
ultimately measure your maturity. Read through these character confessions
and see if they are evidenced in your life:

• I apply God's Word to every situation (Josh. 1:7; Ps. 119;
    2 Tim. 3:15–17).

• I pray more than I complain (Dan. 6:10; Acts 1:14; Eph. 6:18).

• I find it easy to serve others (Matt. 20:28; John 13:4–17; Phil. 2:4).

• I enjoy helping those in need (Matt. 18:33; Luke 10:25–37).

• I am a good example to those around me (1 Cor. 11:1; Rev. 12:11).

• I am submissive and loyal to authority figures (Matt. 8:8–9; Eph. 6:5–8).

• I have a great attitude toward life and its circumstances (Phil. 4:11–13;
    1 Tim. 6:16).

• I am not easily offended (Prov. 14:29, 19:11).

• I am part of the solution, not the problem (Prov. 1:5, 9:9, 11:14).

• I like to give more than receive (Is. 32:8; Acts 20:35; 2 Cor. 9:6–8).

• My finances are in order (Prov. 6:6–11; 1 Cor. 4:2; 2 Cor. 9:10–11).

• I abstain from damaging addictions (Gal. 5:16–23; 1 John 2:15–17).

• I am constantly working to change bad habits (Rom. 6:12–14; Col. 3:8).

• I am able to overcome compromising thoughts and temptations (Rom. 12:2; 2 Cor. 10:5).

• My priorities are in order (Matt. 6:19-21, 33; John 6:27).

• I strive to live humbly (Phil. 2:3–4; James 4:6–7).

## Determining Your Maturity Level

With these thoughts fresh in your mind, **turn now to Part Four, page 207 ("Discerning Your Spiritual Maturity"), the self-discovery exercise on spiritual maturity.** This particular tool will be helpful in determining the strengths and weaknesses of your spiritual growth. If you are serious about growing to new levels of spiritual health and maturity in Christ, use this opportunity to put together some growth goals and disciplines that will enhance your journey. Once you've completed the spiritual maturity exercise, please return to this page and finish reading this chapter.

## Assessing Your Spiritual Maturity

If you were honest with yourself, you probably found the spiritual maturity exercise pretty revealing. Don't underestimate the results and don't lose heart! Each of us has areas that need attention. Regardless of what you discovered about your spiritual maturity, the real test will be what you do to move forward and strengthen your areas of weakness. Here are eight steps you might consider:

### Step One: Recognize Your Weaknesses and Confess Them

"If we confess our sins, he is faithful and just and will forgive us our sins and purify us from all unrighteousness" (1 John 1:9, TNIV).

Before anyone can overcome a weakness, defeat a bad habit, or correct a character flaw, they must be honest with themselves and recognize their shortcomings are not God's intended plan for their life. The willingness to recognize these weaknesses and confess them must be done from a sincere, godly conviction not a compulsion, vain babbling, or coaxing of others. You must see it before God as a wrong course for your life, one that holds you back from fulfilling your purpose.

### Step Two: Pray for God's Assistance

Prayer is our most powerful weapon for change. When we recognize an area that we need to develop or change, but have possibly struggled in the past to move forward, prayer is our partner for breakthrough. "Let us then approach God's throne of grace with confidence, so that we may receive mercy and find grace to help us in our time of need" (Heb. 4:16, TNIV).

**GOD IS TOTALLY WILLING AND ABLE TO HELP YOU, IF YOU JUST GIVE HIM A CHANCE.**

God is not going to hurt you; He wants to help you. Whether you realize it or not, He's on your side! God is totally willing and able to help you, if you just give Him a chance. When we allow Him to fight with us, we have a much better chance of winning. God has never lost a battle.

### Step Three: Look to God's Word for Direction

Once you have confessed and asked for God's assistance through prayer, turn to His Word for guidance and direction. The Bible is God's primary agent for change. His Word can and will change the way you think (your mind), the way you act (your will), and the way you feel (your emotions), ultimately affecting your character. Eventually, this will result in maximizing your maturity.

Many people minimize the Word and its powerful shaping effect in our lives. The writer of Hebrews raised a challenge to revisit the power of God's Word: "God means what he says. What he says goes. His powerful Word is sharp as a surgeon's scalpel, cutting through everything, whether doubt or defense, laying us open to listen and obey. Nothing and no one is impervious to God's Word. We can't get away from it—no matter what" (Heb. 4:12–13, MSG). The longest chapter in the Bible is devoted to the power of God's Word, and the central theme is, "How can a young person live a clean life? By carefully reading the map of your Word ... I delight far more in what you tell me about living than in gathering a pile of riches. I ponder every morsel of wisdom from you … I relish everything you've told me of life, I won't forget a word of it" (Ps. 119:9, 14, MSG).

Take the time to find Scriptures that pertain to certain areas where you want to see growth. Memorize them, meditate on them, believe them … and do them. The Word will change you.

### Step Four: Put Together a Plan to Change

Repentance is not just confession, but also a positive change in behavior. Without that action, weaknesses or habits will persist. Discipline means being able to put off what you want now in exchange for what you want—or need—later.

In Colossians 3:8 Paul challenged the church to put off old behaviors and character habits and exchange them for new ones. "It wasn't long ago that you were doing all that stuff and not knowing any better. But you know better now, so make sure it's all gone for good" (MSG). Decide now to make the changes necessary so you can grow and become what you are intended to be.

### Step Five: Lean on the Holy Spirit to Help

You're halfway there! We've confessed, prayed, introduced God's Word to the situation, and made the decision to change. Our next step is to align our lives to live a Spirit-filled, Spirit-focused life.

**DISCIPLINE MEANS BEING ABLE TO PUT OFF WHAT YOU WANT NOW IN EXCHANGE FOR WHAT YOU WANT—OR NEED—LATER.**

In Galatians 5:16–18 Paul dispensed some simple yet profound wisdom about living a Spirit-filled, Spirit-focused life. "So I say, walk by the Spirit, and you will not gratify the desires of the sinful nature. For the sinful nature desires what is contrary to the Spirit, and the Spirit what is contrary to the sinful nature. They are in conflict with each other, so that you are not to do whatever you want. But if you are led by the Spirit, you are not under the law" (TNIV).

Create a lifestyle that is conducive to the Holy Spirit! Start your day by asking the Holy Spirit to guide your thoughts and actions throughout the day. Speak to Him often and ask Him to direct your steps. Lean on Him for wisdom and discernment in every situation. And when the day is done, ask Him to watch over your dreams as you sleep.

## Step Six: Be Accountable to Someone Who Will Challenge You

You may have failed in the past in some of the areas you have identified. Find someone you're willing to submit to for accountability. You have the potential to be far more successful if you submit yourself and your situation to someone else. Ecclesiastes 4:12 drives home this truth. "Though one may be overpowered, two can defend themselves. A cord of three strands is not quickly broken" (TNIV).

If you're struggling in the area of finances, ask someone you respect to assist you with keeping your budget on track. If you have a difficult time getting up in the morning to spend time with the Lord, ask a friend to call and wake you up. If you are struggling with Internet pornography, sign up for *www.covenanteyes.com* and get someone involved in everything you are watching.

## Step Seven: Hang Around Healthy People

My good friend Gary Beasley used to tell me, "Be careful whom you are following; you may turn out just like them." This catchy phrase has proven true in my life and has been positively responsible for allowing me to increase the pace of my spiritual growth. Paul wrote in 1 Corinthians 15:33–34, "Do not be misled: 'Bad company corrupts good character.'" The reverse is true as well; godly people influence godly behavior.

For many years I met with a group of young men who have all become very dear friends and great men of God. One of our early-morning rituals was to sit around the room and ask ourselves seven accountability questions. I don't know where these originated, but they definitely worked wonders in the lives of these young men to move them into greater areas of spiritual growth, health, and maturity:

**Seven Covenant Questions:**

**1.** Did you spend adequate time in prayer and the Word every day this week?

**2.** Did you spend quality time with your family and children this week?

**3.** Did you expose yourself to any explicit literature or videos this week?

**4.** Did you put yourself in a compromising situation with a person of the opposite sex?

**5.** Did you uphold the mandate of your calling to the best of your ability?

**6.** Did you maintain financial integrity in all of your endeavors?

**7.** Did you just lie to me in any of the previous six questions?

### Step Eight: Persevere

We spend a great deal of time working to change our character, often without seeing much tangible result. However, God sees every step we make. There comes a time when He sees that we are fully able to handle the responsibility and influence, and He quickly unleashes His favor and blessing in our lives. The Bible brings great encouragement to those who feel weary in doing well: "And as for you, brothers and sisters, never tire of doing what is good" (2 Thess. 3:13, TNIV). It also says, "No matter how many times you trip them up, God-loyal people don't stay down long; soon they're up on their feet, while the wicked end up flat on their faces" (Prov. 24:16, MSG).

Never give up moving forward in God. Your spiritual growth and maturity are critical to you fulfilling your destiny. Trials will come and disappointments are certain. There will be times when you grow weak, but you must fight for strength. God will be there for you and give you everything you need to succeed.

> **"DO NOT BE MISLED: 'BAD COMPANY CORRUPTS GOOD CHARACTER.'"**
> **–1 CORINTHIANS 15:33–34, TNIV**

Spiritual maturity isn't some daunting thing you have to strive to *do*; it's a natural progression of living a life of unswerving commitment to God. It's what happens when God plants you in a local church, feeds you with His Word, waters you with His Spirit, and exposes you to the life-giving goodness of the Son. When this happens, you can't help but mature. As you continue to figure out who you are and where you're going, spiritual maturity will help you get there.

# CHAPTER ELEVEN

# SPINNING PLATES
## ADJUSTING YOUR PRIORITIES FOR KINGDOM USE

> "Lord, remind me how brief my time on earth will
> be. Remind me that my days are numbered, and
> that my life is fleeing away. My life is no longer
> than the width of my hand. An entire lifetime is
> just a moment to you; human existence is
> but a breath."
>
> —Psalm 39:4–5, NLT

**M**ike White is one of the most productive and disciplined individuals on the planet. He doesn't have some extraordinary gift or unusual deposit of talent, but rather his tenacious discipline to focus on what really matters most—godly priorities—has helped him to excel.

"I've often been asked, how do you balance or prioritize so many important responsibilities in your life? I run a business, I have pastoral responsibilities over 550 people, I'm involved in the leadership of several influential nonprofit ministries, I'm deeply involved in my three children's lives and schools, I have a great marriage, I maintain a healthy devotional life, I keep my finances in order, I exercise regularly, and I keep a vibrant social life."

So what's his secret? The answer is simple: focus. Although Mike's list of responsibilities may seem unattainable, he has demonstrated that with great focus come great results. Our lives are chock-full of activity, but how much of it is really necessary?

Indeed, Mike does a lot! But you may be surprised at how much he *doesn't* do. He focuses on the few things that matter most. He understands this principle mentioned repeatedly by Jesus: "Whoever can be trusted with very little can also be trusted with much" (Luke 16:10, TNIV).

"My calling as a Christian citizen is deeply important to me," Mike says. "My understanding of the Bible leads me to believe that Christians should influence the culture in which they live, and not the other way around." Mike lives out this conviction and has made it a priority in his life. There isn't much time left for frivolous, non-purposeful activities.

Mike is a man who has chosen to focus on life's most important priorities. "I live by the conviction that my personal destiny is fulfilled one hour at a time. There are things that only I can do; only I can be my wife's husband, or my kids' dad. I focus on my priorities. That means I have to pay attention to them, or they won't have the desired results." Simple, yet profound. This principle applies to all of us.[1]

---

## What's the Most Important?

How would you describe your quality of life? Are you happy with your results so far? If you were to sit down and make a list of those things you believe are most important in your life, what would your list look like? Hopefully, most people would create a list that would include the following priorities: God, family, relationships, personal health and fitness, career, ministry, and finances.

Now let's consider a second list. Think back over the past few weeks and where you *actually* have spent your time—not where you intended to or desired to. Would this second list match your first list? If you're like most people, your actions often don't calibrate perfectly with your intentions. Let's face it; life is complex.

Back in the day, before most of us were old enough to turn on the TV, there was this guy on the Johnny Carson show who was sort of a regular. He would set plates spinning at the top of these rods standing up on end on the stage. His big talent in life was that he could get a dozen or so of these plates spinning at once, but they all required maintenance; he had to keep them spinning or they'd slow down and fall, so he'd race back and forth, spinning each plate like a madman. And the audience would go wild watching him until finally, CRASH! He couldn't keep the plates going, and they'd hit the floor in a fantastic cabaret of shattering racket.

Similarly, just trying to keep the plates spinning in our lives (especially the right ones) can be overwhelming, much less "doing something big for God." We all *intend* to do great things for God, but the reality of daily pressures—holding down a job, taking care of the kids, mowing the lawn, washing the dishes, doing the laundry, changing the oil, spending time with the in-laws—can crash anybody's plate-spinning performance! Before you know it, there's no time left for life's most important priorities.

We don't intend to get distracted; it just happens … life happens! It's no wonder the writer of Hebrews warned, "It's crucial that we keep a firm grip on what we've heard so that we don't drift off" (Heb. 2:1, MSG). It is unfortunate how quickly those unimportant daily pressures dilute our priorities list, causing us to veer off our desired course.

Priorities are important to God; therefore they should be important to us as well. Jesus said, "And he will give you all you need from day to day if you live for him and make the Kingdom of God your primary concern" (Matt. 6:33, NLT). He made it pretty simple: major on the majors, minor on the minors; make your priorities a priority; get them straight and God takes care of the rest.

**NO GREAT MAN OR WOMAN HAS EVER BUILT A SPIRITUAL LEGACY ON GREAT INTENTIONS, BUT RATHER WITH STRATEGIC, DEVOTED ACTION TO GOD AND HIS PURPOSES.**

Where you spend your time has a lot to do with whether or not you reach your God-intended destiny. If your focus is on building your own kingdom, it's unlikely you'll be used much to build His kingdom. No great man or woman has ever built a spiritual legacy on great intentions, but rather with strategic, devoted action to God and His purposes.

Of course, there are certain responsibilities in life that we all must embrace, and those will need some time and attention. And we are typically prone to adding other "responsibilities" that may not be in our best interest. With only twenty-four hours in a day, it comes down to choosing which things are most important and which ones rob us of the precious time we have available.

## Choose Your Priorities: The Choice Is Yours

When I was a child, my grandparents' front living room was filled with beautiful, very expensive white furniture … and it was completely covered in plastic! I can still remember the smell. No one was ever allowed in that room; it was reserved for those special occasions. That beautiful furniture remained enshrined under plastic for years. Its purpose might as well have been for anchoring a small fleet of ships because my grandparents eventually died without ever using this room, or that furniture.

There are many people whose lives are similar to my grandparents' white furniture. They're elegantly handcrafted by the Creator of the universe, but smothered in the plastic of our fleeting, temporary priorities. Deep down, we might have the greatest intention of using our specially crafted lives for God's glory one of these days. But days have turned into weeks and, for some of us, years. We need to pull the plastic off and use our lives for their intended purpose.

When I reflect back on the story of Mike White, I am challenged (and perplexed) by the way one individual can consistently accomplish so much. I don't want to admit that it might be his discipline to focus on high priorities, and so I allow my mind to wander aimlessly, soothing the emotions, hoping I can keep just a few worthless habits. Does he have some secret insider status with God? Maybe he has twenty or thirty full-time assistants at his every beck and call? The answer to these questions is no. And the answer isn't found in his wallet, either.

God has a way of bringing me back to reality and forcing me to assess my situation, reminding me that He gave me an equal share of the two precious commodities involved in Mike's influence and success: time and freedom of choice.

Those two basic components have been put in your lap as well. Each of us has been given twenty-four hours in a day. That's why the Bible says to "make the most of every opportunity" (Eph. 5:16; Col 4:5, TNIV). What you do with those 1,440 minutes every day is your choice. God gave you a free will. These precious commodities were given with the intention that we use them wisely.

Many Christians spend more time watching television than praying. So maybe the best thing to do is just give up trying and join the Coach Potato Marathon. (This is no joke—it's an actual event.) *U.S. News & World Report* gave a snapshot into this relatively uneventful event:

> On your mark, get set, loaf! This year's Coach Potato Marathon got off in true sedentary style with contestants relaxing on a well-worn couch and watching a videotape of the course they did not run. Participants in Sunday's non-marathon collected pledges for each of the twenty-six miles of open highway none would ever jog ... Couches were parked in front of the television set. On the screen was the course video, with a red arrow pointing to the center of the screen that said, "You are not here." Mary Hamilton, the program coordinator said the event was to raise finances for the city's homeless shelter. Their first thought was to run a marathon, but as Mrs. Hamilton put it, "That's too much work for us."[2]

Fortunately our lives were meant for so much more. Our responsibility is to take the time we have been given and our freedom to choose and use our lives for God's glory. The Bible challenges us in this endeavor, in Ephesians 5:16–17: "So watch your step. Use your head. Make the most of every chance you get. These are desperate times! Don't live carelessly, unthinkingly. Make sure you understand what the Master wants" (MSG).

Here, Paul is challenging us to stop, pause, reflect, and make sure that we are thinking straight about how we use our time. Our actions should be aligned to God's intentions for our life, not our own. Time is short ... and important. Removing careless priorities and replacing them with important ones is critical.

Vaclav Havel, a former president of the Czech Republic, reiterates this point: "The real test of a man is not when he plays the role that he wants for himself, but when he plays the role destiny has for him."[3] God doesn't want us to forget the reason for our existence or waste any time fulfilling it. He wants every minute we've been given to be a minute well spent. He wants our priorities to be in order. We should take the advice of the prophet Jeremiah—"Let's take a good look at the way we're living and reorder our lives under God" (Lam. 3:40, MSG)—and make some needed priority adjustments.

## What Are Your Priorities?

If we fail to give our highest priorities our greatest attention, something of lesser significance will quickly take their place and fill up our time. We must be very intentional in identifying and protecting life's most important priorities.

It would be impossible to develop a priority list that fits every person, and it would even be contradictory to the message of this book. You are unique and special and have been created by God for a very special and specific purpose. That means there are some things that might be a very high priority in your life, whereas that same item in another person's life might be a diversion from their true purpose. However, there are a few priorities that should be considered non-negotiable facts of life. These include:

- Your relationship with God (Matt. 22:37).
- Fulfilling the purposes of God in your life (Gen. 1:26–28).
- A lifestyle of loving others and loving yourself (Matt. 22:39).
- Becoming more like Christ, possessing godly character (Gal. 5:22–23).
- A dedication and commitment to vital relationships (Eph. 5:21–6:4).
- Sharing your faith with unsaved people (Matt. 28:19–20).
- Discipling others to be like Christ (Matt. 28:20).
- Financial stewardship (Mal. 3:8–10; Mark 12:41–44; 2 Cor. 8:2–7).
- Personal health, hygiene, and fitness (1 Cor. 6:19–20).
- Dedication to work and excellence (Eph. 6:5–9; Col. 3:23).
- Adequate rest and sleep (Ps. 91:1, 139:3; Eccles. 5:12; Heb. 4:1).

## Measuring Your Priorities

After reading through the list above, can you say that your life contains important priorities or time-robbers? The goal of this chapter is not to make you feel bad about how you spend your time and attention, but to inspire you to consider how you approach the significant priorities of life.

There are two different self-discovery exercises in Part Four for this chapter: "Making Priority Adjustments" and "Reviewing Your Schedule." The priority exercise is an opportunity for you to evaluate how much actual time you spend each week in the eleven main priority areas. **Turn to page 211 for the priority exercise.**

The availability worksheet is helpful once you've adjusted your priorities to determine when you can devote time to serving in your local church. Once you've aligned your priorities, you'll know how much time you can commit and what days you are available to serve. **You will find the availability worksheet on page 213.**

Once you have completed both exercises, you can return to this page and finish reading the rest of this chapter.

## Making the Shift

There comes a point in our lives when we realize those things that always seemed to be most important and took all of our time and resources are now dwarfed by the realization that life is short and time is precious. One of the greatest excerpts in all of Scripture comes from a man sitting in prison, reflecting back on his life and all of his accomplishments. Much like King Solomon of old, the apostle Paul came to realize that all of his previous priorities really meant nothing in the larger scope of life. He devoted

Hopefully, you took the challenge seriously and have prayerfully considered making some adjustments to your priorities. Some of us might need to make only minor adjustments, while others might need to completely stop the plates we're spinning and start over with a whole new set. In either case, the goal is to align the time we have been entrusted with God's purposes for our lives. This is the Paul's admonition: "Make the most of every opportunity" (Col. 4:5, TNIV).

Find the balance between what is idealistic and what is realistic. You may have felt the tension while scoring your priority exercise. On one hand, you have a desire to get more involved in a certain area of ministry, but you have other priorities taking up all your time and attention. There are times and seasons when certain priorities need special attention. King Solomon said, "There is a time for everything, and a season for every activity under the heavens" (Eccles. 3:1, TNIV). If it applied to a king who had everything, it probably applies to you.

Make sure you're making the necessary changes while finding balance in all you do.

much of his life to building his education so he could be known as a "Pharisee of Pharisees." He actually took the lives of those who were following Christ so he could build his reputation and gain greater influence. He even bragged about his strong family lineage that caused him to be classified as one of society's most elite. And then it happened. God revealed His great truth and changed Paul's life—and his priorities—forever.

In a damp, darkened prison cell, his legs shackled and fortified guards standing close by, Paul wrote,

> The very credentials these people are waving around as something special, I'm tearing up and throwing out with the trash—along with everything else I used to take credit for. And why? Because of Christ. Yes, all the things I once thought were so important are gone from my life. Compared to the high privilege of knowing Christ Jesus as my Master, firsthand, everything I once thought I had going for me is insignificant—dog dung. I've dumped it all in the trash so that I could embrace Christ and be embraced by him. (Phil. 3:7–9, MSG)

Paul's greatest challenge came in making the decision to change his priorities. What used to be important to him, he later considered dog dung. Thank God, he made the shift!

The hardest part of change is deciding to actually do it. Once you've made up your mind, the details fall into place. Changing your priorities will take some effort, but it is well worth the cost. Here are some tips that might help:

**Get God's Help from the Start**
"With God, all things are possible" (Matt. 19:26, TNIV). This includes some of the more difficult shifts in priorities. Look at your priority exercise and invite God to be involved in each of these areas. Jesus promised, "Ask and it will be given to you" (Luke 11:9, TNIV). Regardless of how difficult the shift might be, all things are possible with God if we ask Him to help us from the start.

**Set Realistic Goals**
Once you've identified areas you want to change, set some very tangible, reachable, and realistic goals. "Write what you see. Write it out in big block letters so that it can be read on the run" (Hab. 2:2, MSG). Something happens when you sit down and write out your goals. For instance, if you want to

recommit yourself to personal devotions, set a goal to get up at a certain time each morning to read and pray. If you feel you need to share your faith with someone, make it your goal to share at least one encouraging thought with someone every day. For each priority you want to change, set at least one realistic goal for that change. Hold yourself to it and make it a new priority. It is always better to prepare and prevent, rather than repair and repent.

**Protect Your Personal Time**

At first this may sound a bit selfish. But even Jesus understood the value of this priority. He often woke early in the morning to be alone with His Father.

In East Malaysia, during a worship service, a teenage girl shared her faith and was then baptized in the baptistry. While all this was going on, a pastor noticed some worn-out luggage leaning against the wall. He asked a church member for an explanation of the suitcase. He pointed to the girl who had just been baptized and said, "Her father said if she was baptized as a Christian, she could never go home again."[4] She was determined to make God number one in her life, which meant being willing to make a hard choice.

He went into the wilderness alone. He went up on the hillside alone. He took off on solo boat trips. He took a walk on the water alone. Jesus understood that there was a need to have His time alone.

There are a few things that only you can do for yourself. If you allow others to dictate your life and schedule, you will never find the time to relax, reflect, and be refreshed. At this moment, my cell phone has five voicemails, my work phone has four voicemails,

**THE HARDEST PART OF CHANGE IS DECIDING TO ACTUALLY DO IT.**

and my inbox has sixteen unread messages … and I don't feel guilty at all. I'll take time to answer each of these, but I live under the principle that people don't take my time … I give it to them.

**Learn to Delegate**

Try not to be the person who has to do everything for everyone. Those who have to be involved in doing everything never have enough time to realistically accomplish anything. Certain responsibilities and tasks are important, but the next time something comes your way, ask yourself two questions: "Does this task help or hurt me with my priorities?" and "Is there someone else who could do this task?" Give yourself a break … give that task away!

### Learn to Say No

There are times when the word *no* is appropriate. Please don't use this as a license to say no to everything that comes your way, but understand that in certain circumstances, there may be a justified occasion to decline. If someone asks you to serve in a particular area and you're overloaded with higher priorities, it's okay to say, "I would love to help with that, but right now my plate is full. I hope you understand."

> **"EFFICIENCY IS DOING THINGS RIGHT; EFFECTIVENESS IS DOING THE RIGHT THINGS."**
> —PETER DRUCKER

In other cases, you may find conflicts between what you *should* do and what you'd *like* to do. For instance, let's say you've made a new commitment to serve in your church, and, in a recent conversation with your pastor, you promised you would assist him at the men's breakfast on Saturday. The moment you hang up the phone, you get another call from your work buddy who has an extra ticket to a baseball game … front row, right behind first base. Of course, you want to renege on your offer to serve and catch the game instead, but baseball will have to wait until next time; you've made a prior commitment. Remember these words from the late Peter Drucker, known as one of the greatest writers, thinkers, and business consultants of his time: "Efficiency is doing things right; effectiveness is doing the right things."[5]

### Set Limits

Rome wasn't built in a day, and neither is your life. Your realistic goals must have limits. If you're making the decision to cut back on work, go home on time. If you want to cut back on TV, set a time limit—maybe one hour per day—and stick to it.

### Downsize Your Life

I recently saw a bumper sticker that said, "The person with the most toys wins … but he's dead and broke." How true! We spend our lives acquiring and fail to realize how much more we're actually losing. You might be gaining things that seem important now, but there will come a time when you'll have to set a limit for how much you will allow to be piled on your shoulders. Just how many plates do you think you can spin at once, anyway?

You may be very successful in business and find yourself involved in three or four business ventures. Maybe you're very gifted in hospitality and are coordinating every social event in your church. You might have been blessed financially so you have a third home, a fourth car, a new boat, and … the list goes on. There comes a time when we have to assess all of life's responsibilities and possessions, and downsize in order to free up the time and energy needed for the things that are most important.

## Don't Lose the Joy
Are you happy in all you do? Do you find joy in the time you give to your priorities? Life can be tough, but don't be misled: life should be enjoyable also. I'm a firm believer that happiness is a choice! Television anchor Hugh Downs said it best: "A happy person is not a person in a certain set of circumstances but rather a person with a certain set of attitudes."[6]

## Avoid Burnout
One of the greatest deterrents to fulfilling your purpose is fatigue. When you feel yourself becoming weary and tired, take a break. Even God took a break when He created the world. "So on the seventh day he rested from all his work" (Gen. 2:2, TNIV). If God can take a break, so can you.

Schedule frequents times during the week when you can refuel your body. Enjoy yourself. Watch a movie. Go to the gym and work out. Sleep in. Pull weeds in the yard. Only you know what activities will rejuvenate you.

## Reassess Your Life Regularly
You can only expect what you inspect. Frequent times of reassessment are necessary to ensure you stay on track. It is easy to veer off course ever so slightly. A commercial pilot friend of mine mentioned once said that the typical flight from New York to Hawaii is off course 90 percent of the time, requiring constant assessment and adjustments. Life is much the same way. Frequent adjustments are necessary to stay on our God-intended course.

Once there was a Christian businessman from America traveling to India on a short-term missionary trip. On one particular day during his journey he found himself at a leper colony. Outside the walls of this leprosarium he observed a beautiful sight; a young missionary nurse was smiling and singing while attending to the desperate needs of a filthy, wretched, leprous Indian beggar. The businessman has his camera around his neck but couldn't get up the nerve to take a picture. He paused, took a few steps back, and, with tears filling his eyes, said, "Ma'am, I wouldn't do that for a million dollars!" The lady turned and smiled, replying, "Neither would I."[7]

# PART THREE

## MAKING LIFE MATTER

## CHAPTER TWELVE

# HERE COMES THE BRIDE
## THE LOCAL CHURCH: GOD'S DIVINE INSTRUMENT

> "This is the rock on which I will put together my
> church, a church so expansive with energy that not
> even the gates of hell will be able to keep it out.
> And that's not all. You will have complete and free
> access to God's kingdom, keys to open any and
> every door: no more barriers between heaven and
> earth, earth and heaven."
>
> —Matthew 16:17–19, MSG

One glance at Jeanette Moore and her son Nicky, and you'd probably think that this is the happiest little family on earth. They giggle and play; Nicky smiles and Jeanette's heart swells. They have so much to be happy about—but not that long ago, Jeanette could only hope that she and Nicky would be together. Their story has been fraught with heart-wrenching obstacles and a lot of pain, but Jeanette placed her future in God's hands, and somewhere along the way, they found their miracle.

The first of several consecutive tragedies in Jeanette's life came when her husband was diagnosed with severe mental illness, which choked the life out of their marriage, causing it to rapidly collapse. Her attachment to the Jehovah's Witnesses faith fell short of meeting her spiritual and emotional needs. Because of her failed marriage and subsequent divorce, the church abandoned her on the doorsteps of solitude without any support during this difficult time. "The time when I needed the church most was when I received what I needed least: excommunication," she says. "I'll never forget the hopelessness I felt, cut off from my family, friends, and church, left to fend for myself when I was broken and alone."

How could a church that was supposed to love and care for people become so ugly and damaging? Layer upon layer of hurt and sorrow began to encrust Jeanette's broken heart, yielding deep-rooted revulsion for the church and leaving her desperate to find someone who cared.

Jeanette eventually met a man who became her second husband. It had been more than four years since she last stepped into a church. She hoped this new marriage would fill some of the emptiness she felt. Before long, Jeanette's second marriage began to collapse as well. Her husband was sent to prison, leaving her to fend for herself again, this time with their son Nicky. She felt the familiar pain of being alone, desperate, out of money, and out of hope.

"Just when I thought things couldn't get any worse, Nicky was diagnosed with acute lymphoblastic leukemia." Jeanette had no insurance, very little money, and not a family member in sight to help her deal with the overwhelming thought of losing her son. It drove her deep into depression.

But somehow God knew just what she needed most. Help was on the way.

"There were a bunch of guys that I had met at work, and they kept telling me about their church. As far as I was concerned, church was a place where you were controlled and filled with fear, and the last thing I needed was gasoline thrown on my raging pile of problems. But these guys seemed different; something about them was so happy, enjoyable, encouraging, and always hopeful."

Finally Jeanette gave the church a shot, and on her first visit, she picked up a book written by one of the pastors. She thought, "Could this be the God I'm really looking for?" Skeptical yet determined, she stuck with it, and that first Sunday became two, then three, then nine. Jeanette was convinced this was for real—she couldn't explain it, but she knew it was true.

"I don't know how to put it into words," she says, holding back tears. "All my life I thought church was this controlling, non-relational institution. But at the lowest part of my life, I was introduced to a church—a warm family of people—that loved me when I couldn't give anything in return. They became my strength, my support, my saving grace."

Over the coming months, Jeanette's church family rolled up their sleeves and made sure that she and Nicky had all the food they needed. "Boxes of food came and kept coming, then they sent a Thanksgiving turkey, then Christmas presents, and, most of all, financial support. I remember having no money for my son's medicine, and the church stepped in to pay for every dime."

The story of Jeanette and Nicky is exactly what church is about. Someone reached out to her and told her about a spiritual family (not a building) that loved her and would help her. Consequently, she discovered the Word of God, which encouraged her and lifted her spirit. The Spirit of God came and gave her hope and direction. Her ability to lift her heart and her hands during worship filled her soul with thankfulness. Her small group and new friends surrounded her, prayed for her, and met some pretty significant needs. Her pastors gave her counsel regarding some life-changing decisions. Both she and her son are growing and being discipled. She's learning how to live a victorious, abundant life as a part of the family of God.

When asked what her church means to her, Jeanette smiles and says, "The church is my everything. It's my place of strength, it's my family, it's my support ... I would have never made it without the church."[1]

---

## What Is Church?

Your definition of church and actual involvement (or lack thereof) will have a massive effect on your purpose. Despite the many opinions floating around today about church and its validity, we should all agree that our opinions are dwarfed by what God thinks about the role that church should play in the life of every believer.

**YOUR DEFINITION OF CHURCH AND ACTUAL INVOLVEMENT (OR LACK THEREOF) WILL HAVE A MASSIVE EFFECT ON YOUR PURPOSE.**

The church isn't a building, nor is it a club or committee. It isn't man-made, and it isn't defined on man's terms. The church isn't some parenthetical revelation that God came up with because our forefathers couldn't get their act together. The Church is the bride of Christ. It is the sovereign will of God and the central fact of His will. From the very begin-

ning, God dreamed of a Church, He desired a Church, He willed a Church
… and He will have His Church. So let's put some legs to the term.

The word *church* is derived from the Greek word *ekklesia*, which is made up of
two other words: *ek*, which means "out of" and *kaleo*, which means "to call."
Thus the word church literally means "the called-out ones."

But called out for what purpose?

In his book, *The Church in the New Testament*, Kevin Conner writes, "The
Church, the Assembly, the Congregation were not just 'called-out ones,' but
'called out to assemble together.'"[2] In essence, the Church is a body of believers that God has called out of the darkness of this world and assembled together as one spiritual family; they learn and apply the Word of God to every
aspect of their lives, worshiping Him in spirit and truth, devoting themselves
to one another and to reaching those who don't yet know Christ.

It is important to point out the two references of church in Scripture: the
Church Universal (or body of Christ) and the local church. Many believe
purpose is found in "the body of Christ" only and not necessarily in a local
church.

**The Universal Church**
The body of Christ spans the globe and has literally invaded almost every
nation and people group. It's an awesome thing to consider that we're part of
the largest network of people on the face of the planet. The universal Church
stretches beyond denominational lines, age, race, culture, and time. In fact,
we're even part of all those who have gone before us (Heb. 12:1–2), who are
counting on us to be part of ushering in the return of the King.

**THERE CANNOT BE THE UNIVERSAL CHURCH WITHOUT THE LOCAL CHURCH.**

In Matthew 16:18 Jesus is talking
about the Church universal: "On
this rock I will build my church,
and the gates of death will not
overcome it" (TNIV). He will
build His Church, a global Church that will be vibrant and victorious. It will
span every tongue, tribe, and nation. It will expand through the generations
and reach to the ends of the earth. God's people, the universal Church, are
everywhere.

## The Local Church

There cannot be the universal Church without the local church; the universal Church is mainly comprised of millions of local churches. The Bible confirms this with the ongoing use of the term *church*, which is used some 114 times. Ninety-six references are clearly to the local church.[3] In Matthew 18:15–20, Jesus gives instruction on how to properly deal with offenses in the church. It is clear that discipline must involve some form of leadership, direction, accountability, understanding of the issues, and overseeing of the process on a localized level. We would be hard-pressed to see the requirements Jesus defines practically carried out in the context of the universal Church. This is not to say that these principles don't still apply to the universal Church; however, we come to the logical conclusion that it would be impossible to carry this particular process out without the involvement of the local church. This is only one of the many reasons why the local church exists!

God needs the local church. The task of the local church is to care for people. Here we are encouraged and exhorted, built up and humbled, loved and disciplined. We meet with God and meet with others. We learn about His Word and about ourselves. We overcome darkness in our own lives, while helping others to overcome the darkness in theirs. Is there any other place that will do all of that for you?

A few years ago I spent some time in the Philippines. I took a jumbo jet thousands of miles across the Pacific Ocean, rode in a Jeep eighteen hours out into the Camarines Norte region to the town of Labo, then flagged down a three-wheeled tricycle taxi that took me to a small, modest home where these wonderful people welcomed me and hosted me for weeks. The climate was a world away from what I was used to; the food was ... well, let's say it was "distinctive"; their culture was richly unique; their lifestyle was laid back with no running water and no electricity; the language was difficult to learn and almost impossible to understand. Everything about that place was different, different, different! However, *one* thing was the same: God's presence. I vividly remember the first sentence in the song, "Buhay, buhay, buhay magpakailan man. Aking Hesus ay buhay. Buhay magpakailan man." ("Alive, alive, alive forever more. My Jesus is alive, alive forevermore.") We were unable to communicate the whereabouts of the nearest restroom without engaging in a full-on game of Charades, yet we were infatuated together with the presence of God. For the first time in my life, I understood how local churches have been divinely placed around the world to reach people. I understood that, just like me, my Filipino friends were Christians redeemed by the same blood of Christ, serving the same God and ultimate purpose. The universal Church became real to me.

## So What's the Problem?

Why do so many people have a problem with the church? There are two main groups who struggle with it: those who don't attend and those who attend but misunderstand the important role the church plays in their lives. Let's step into their worlds for a moment.

### Those Who Don't Attend Church

According to a 2006 survey, there are 298,444,215 people living in the United States.[4] Researcher George Barna reports that 85 percent of those identify themselves as Christians, yet only 45 percent say they attend church regularly, leaving 164,144,318 who are not attending church at all.[5] In fact, Barna states that the number of unchurched adults in America has doubled since 1991.[6]

What baffles me is that every one of these people, on some level, wants to figure out who they are and where they're going, yet they choose to ignore (or are simply ignorant to the fact) that it is *in the church* where their ultimate purpose will be fulfilled. Here are eight reasons people often give for not attending church:

1. *"Church is really boring."* The sad part of this statement is that it is partially true. Some churches today start at eleven o'clock sharp and fill their ninety-minute service with activity but no life-giving substance. On the other hand, some churches have a vibrant, life-giving culture. I've always told those who use the boredom excuse, "You'll always get out of it what you put into it." Regardless of the atmosphere of church, there is always the opportunity to change it instead of reacting to it! Take the challenge to make it exciting yourself! Remember, Jesus came to give life abundantly, not sparingly (John 10:10).

2. *"Church is irrelevant."* Unfortunately, this statement can be true as well. Many churches still use archaic methods to reach people. Those same songs they were singing in 1976 ... they're still singing them. Don't get me wrong; I love the golden oldies, too ... but I love them for nostalgic reasons that would mean nothing to today's searching soul. More often than not, yesterday's revolution is out of context today. Cultures change, and so should the church. The apostle Paul said, "I have become all things to all people so that

by all possible means I might save some" (1 Cor. 9:22, TNIV). That doesn't mean you have to abort biblical principles and values; it simply means that you should adapt them to be more relevant to those you intend to reach.

3. *"Church doesn't meet my needs."* In many cases, this frustration is a legitimate concern. Most people who come to church for the first time bring with them what seems to be an entire grab bag full of personal issues that need attention. They aren't looking for a sign-up sheet for the next Sunday school class, but for someone who will help them iron out the warps and wrinkles of their life. They need someone like the Good Samaritan, who found the desperate man half-dead in the ditch. "And when he saw him, he had compassion" (Luke 10:33, NKJV). We have an obligation to reach out to those who need help. They are in every service, and God wants to help them discover their purpose. You can help.

4. *"I don't fit into that church."* Not all people fit into all churches. Each of us is a little different and may require a different kind of church. I know many churches where I absolutely love the people, but the church itself leaves more to be desired. That doesn't mean what they're doing is wrong; it just fits them better than it fits me.

5. *"I don't have any relationships there."* Eighty-six percent of all people who ever visit church and decide to stay do so because they had a relationship connection with someone there *before* they ever attended in the first place.[7] Relationship is key; people knew someone, so they stayed! Likewise, many people attend a church and don't stay simply because nobody reached out to them and they never experienced the joy of building healthy, lasting relationships within the congregation. How sad. If you find yourself in this dilemma, step out and build a relationship with someone at your church. Remember, relationship is a two-way street. If you already are part of a church, reach out and touch someone (sounds like a great advertising idea). New people are counting on you.

6. *"People there have offended me."* Life is full of offenses. It is guaranteed that wherever you go in life, offenses will happen. They'll pop up in your marriage, with your children, or at your job. You'll experience disagreements with your parents, your neighbors, your friends, the guy in the yellow car that cut you off ... even people at church. Offenses happen. In order to repair them you must face them, not run from them. The Bible admonishes,

A few weeks ago, I was in the store trying on some new pants. They looked pretty cool, and I really wanted to get them. I went into the dressing room and tried them on—to my surprise, they didn't fit. "That's it—I'll never wear pants again!" I thought to myself. Okay, that didn't really happen (and I do wear pants, by the way), but you can see how ridiculous that would be. Instead of thrashing about in a tantrum, screaming "never again," I simply tried on another pair of pants. Guess what—they fit like they were made for me. The parallel is obvious: if you've tried church and it didn't fit, go try another one.

"Above all else, guard your heart, for it affects everything you do" (Prov. 4:23, NLT). God knows that dealing with offense is paramount to you having a clean heart. If someone has been offended and therefore leaves the church, they run the risk of turning their back on their Christian family, friends, and maybe even God. Don't let offense run you off.

7. *"I don't see any value in church."* A person with this view of church probably hasn't looked far enough. We perceive many things in life to be without value, not because they actually lack value, but simply because we don't understand them. If God created church and said it was of the utmost importance, we should trust He knows more than us.

8. *"All they talk about at church is money."* Actually, that's all they talk about on the news, in magazines, and in movies. That's all they talk about at the town hall, the mortgage company, and the school board meeting. Why doesn't *that* bother you? Most people talk about money … a lot. So do you! Every day we talk about budgets, salary raises, shopping, expenses, debits, credits, vacations, house projects, gifts, and entertainment. Jesus actually talked about money more than almost any other topic. Please don't misread me; there is a balance. Of course, there's much more to life than money, but money is pretty important. In fact, money has more to do with ministry and carrying out the daily operations of the church than you may realize.

**OFFENSES HAPPEN. IN ORDER TO REPAIR THEM YOU MUST FACE THEM, NOT RUN FROM THEM.**

One of the reasons I believe pastors should talk about money is because so many people today need help with it. Debt is so ingrained into our culture that is seems almost foreign to consider living a debt-free lifestyle. In fact, recent studies show that 70 percent of Americans live paycheck to paycheck. It is no wonder, when we look at the $660 billion Americans owe in credit card debt. I am sure it doesn't help matters that 5.3 billion credit card offers are mailed annually.[8] With the daily barrage hitting us from every angle like a Mack truck, we should talk about ways to be wise stewards of what God has blessed us with.

Finances are a personal matter and should be handled delicately. However, the Bible gives the Church great room to provoke each other to good works, healthy living, financial stewardship and spiritual growth.

**Those Who Attend Church, But Misunderstand Its Importance**
First of all, let me say that I am a firm believer in the local church and that, for the most part, we are successfully gaining ground in regard to the Great Commission to go and make disciples (Matt. 28:19). There are countless thousands of thriving, growing local churches filled with millions of people who have passion and purpose operating in their lives. However, I would be in denial to not recognize that there are many today who attend church but have not grasped the true meaning of church in their lives. If they don't engage wholeheartedly in their local church and begin developing their spiritual gifts,

**WE PERCEIVE MANY THINGS IN LIFE TO BE WITHOUT VALUE, NOT BECAUSE THEY ACTUALLY LACK VALUE, BUT SIMPLY BECAUSE WE DON'T UNDERSTAND THEM.**

talents, and passions, their efforts in life will have been for naught. The Bible says, "If people can't see what God is doing, they stumble all over themselves; but when they attend to what he reveals, they are most blessed" (Prov. 29:18, MSG). People who are thriving in every arena of life are the ones who thrive in the church family. Some common concerns church attenders have about the local church are:

1. *"I attend multiple churches because I enjoy a little variety."* I would be the first to admit that every church can't meet every person's needs. But your spouse can't meet all your needs either. The last thing I would ever do to my wife, who I am faithfully committed to, is tell her, "Honey, I want you to know that I really love you, and you have done such a great job of meeting *most* of my needs. But I have a couple of needs that you haven't been meeting, and let's face it, you probably never will. Now, I don't want you to feel bad,

because it isn't your fault, but I want you to know that I'm going to look for someone else to fill that void on Wednesday nights, someone who can offer something you don't. I'm sure you understand, right?"

I can already hear the wheels turning in your mind. No, my wife isn't my church, but I'm building eternity with a group of people who have become my spiritual family. There are times when I get upset with my spiritual family, but that doesn't mean I move in with another family! Get planted and stick with one church.

For those who are faithfully committed to a local church and, on occasion, attend an event or service at another church, feel free to do so, but be faithful to your home church first.

2. *"I'm leaving that church for another one that's better."* God does move people from one church to another. I have experienced this myself. My family and I have only been involved with two churches ever. Our first church was in Lake Tahoe, California, where my wife and I were saved. We attended and faithfully served there for more than fifteen years; it was the only church family we had ever known. Our time there was one of the most fruitful and special seasons of our life. Our pastors, Terry and Cheryl, were like parents to us, and to this day, we hold them very dear in our hearts.

> **YOUR CHURCH FAMILY IS WHERE MOST OF YOUR LIFE'S PURPOSES ARE DISCOVERED, DEVELOPED, AND DEPLOYED.**

However, God chose to move us to Portland. The Bible says, "In their hearts human beings plan their course, but the Lord establishes their steps" (Prov. 16:9, TNIV). Was it easy? Absolutely not! Was it unequivocally God? Yes! Today, my wife and I are part of a wonderful family at City Bible Church. Our children have found their spouses here, our grandchildren are being raised here, and our eternal destiny is continuing to take shape here. So God does move people.

Many people move to other churches for the wrong reason entirely. There are a variety of reasons you might use to justify your actions, but let me caution you to make sure it is God who is leading you. Make sure it is for the right reason because your church family is where most of your life's purposes are discovered, developed, and deployed. Fulfilling your purpose will take a lifetime, and being part of one church family can make the journey more fulfilling.

3. *"I really don't want to commit, but I do enjoy attending."* I wish every relationship could be that way. Life would be a lot easier if we had the freedom to flit about without so much as a whim of commitment. But the true benefits of relationship never come without true commitment. What brings such depth to the relationships I enjoy with my church family is that we are committed to each other through every circumstance. After all, real love is all about giving, not getting.

4. *"We need to redefine church as we know it."* Let's walk very carefully here. There is a growing trend today where many church leaders are attempting to redefine church to be more relevant to a generation in need of Christ. I would be the first to trumpet the need for innovation and creativity, but not at the expense of exchanging them for the timeless and priceless truths of the Bible. We need to keep our methods current but protect biblical principles. We must be relevant, but not compromise our convictions or morals. I once needed to change my hairdo (at the request of my wife and daughters) and did … but I always need to leave my heart untouched. While many things inside the church today need change, there are others that need to remain the same. Let's give 'er a new hairdo, but leave her foundation intact.

5. *"We have chosen to build our own ministry because the church has failed."* As an executive pastor of a fairly large church, I would be the first to admit there are times when we fail to meet every need, every time, in the right manner, with the right heart, with the right level of intensity. We live in an imperfect world, filled with imperfect people, who make up imperfect churches. We're not yet without spot or wrinkle, but someday we will be.

God's perfect will is that all those who claim to be part of the body of Christ

A man approached the famous Charles Spurgeon after one of his services, disgusted with the condition of the church. He informed Pastor Spurgeon he was out to find the "perfect church," and if he couldn't, he would find another solution. Spurgeon replied, "My church is filled with great people, but there could be a Judas among them. Even Jesus found a few traitors … Sir, my church is not the one you are looking for, but if you happen to find such a church, I beg you to not join it, for you would spoil the whole thing."[9]

(universal) connect themselves with the body of Christ (local) within the context of a local church. Over the years, the Church has failed in some respects to carry out her mission. As a result, a host of caring, loving, passionate visionaries have developed ministries that specialize in meeting the massive needs of the world today (such as missionary societies, evangelism ministries, youth organizations). These groups have had a dramatic impact around the world, touching the lives of millions of people. But I firmly believe this is the Church's responsibility; as the Church becomes all she was intended to be and believers everywhere dedicate themselves wholeheartedly to fulfilling their purpose, the need for these important ministries outside of the local church will diminish.

6. *"The leadership of the church no longer has vision for the church."* This might be perhaps one of the greatest tragedies of all. Many of those who are called to steer the ship have descended to their cabins for a nice long nap. Fortunately, there are multitudes of dynamic, Holy Spirit-led, passionate leaders who are navigating the Church to her intended destination. But that doesn't negate that many churches are shrinking and, in some cases, dying. Every week in America, somewhere between fifty and seventy-five churches close their doors forever.[10] That is as many as 3,900 churches each year. God's purpose is that His church grows and thrives, not dwindles and dies.

As Christians, each of us must make it a priority to pray for our pastors and our church. Pray for the leaders to remain pure, focused, and passionate. Pray for the church to grow in spiritual health and numerical growth. And pray for God's presence and leading to be the driving force in all we do. Not only are we to make our lives count, but God also intends for our churches to count. You were intended to be part of the church, and the church was intended to be part of you. *You* are the church, and *I* am the church. Together we can make our churches count.

> **YOU WERE INTENDED TO BE PART OF THE CHURCH, AND THE CHURCH WAS INTENDED TO BE PART OF YOU.**

In reviewing reasons people leave the local church or are unfaithful, there are some definite reasons to be both concerned and encouraged. It's our responsibility, and should be our passion, to rededicate ourselves to our local churches so we can be examples to all around us—both churched and unchurched—

that God's original blueprint is still valid and functioning. Let's be passionate and excited about the local church!

## Jesus Loves the Church

Before we go any further, pause for a moment and ask yourself these questions: "Do I love my local church?" "How passionately involved am I in both serving and supporting my local church?" Hopefully, these questions are more of an encouragement than an exhortation.

What if we were to ask Jesus the same questions today? "Jesus, do you love the Church?" Scripture answers that one quickly, "Christ loved the church and gave himself up for her" (Eph. 5:25, TNIV). Next question: "Jesus, how passionately are You involved in serving and supporting the local church?" Again, Scripture answers, "Therefore he is able to save completely those who come to God through him, because he always lives to intercede for them" (Heb. 7:25, TNIV).

It seems pretty clear: Jesus died for the Church, and He also lives, always interceding, for her. Jesus loves the Church. As a young boy at the age of twelve, Jesus' parents thought He was lost, so they went on a massive search to find Him. Three days later they found Him. Where? In the Jewish Temple! He said to them, "Why were you searching for me? Didn't you know I had to be in my Father's house?" (Luke 2:49, TNIV). His answer states the obvious.

On many occasions Jesus referred to the Church as His bride. I have been to many weddings in my life, perhaps hundreds. While the crowd stares at the beautiful bride walking down the aisle, my eyes are set on the groom. Oftentimes he is crying, overwhelmed with emotion, as the love of his life walks down the aisle to be presented to him. As an illustration to help us attempt to comprehend Christ's love for the Church, God compares it to a man's love for his bride. In his book, *Stop Dating the Church*, Joshua Harris says, "Is it possible that God didn't get His inspiration for loving the church from marriage, but the one reason He created marriage was to illustrate His love for the church? God invented romance and pursuit and the promise of undying love between man and woman so that throughout our lives we could catch a faint glimmer of the intense love Christ has for those He died to save. What a passion He has for His church. The strongest argument I know for why you and I should love and care about the church is that Jesus does."[11]

Many interpret the passage of Scripture in Ephesians 5:22–33 to be Jesus speaking about the Church (big *C* universal), and I would agree with them. But this must also be interpreted in context to the components that make up the big *C* Church, which is the small *c* local church. Jesus loves His Church, and He loves every local church. We are to love it the same!

## Reasons Why We Need the Church

We are not only to love the church, but we really need the church! Rick Warren says, "A Christian without a church home is like an organ without a body, a sheep without a flock, or a child without a family. It is an unnatural state."[12] Without a local church, our lives are incomplete. You may have needs that aren't being met through your local church, but God intends for it to provide the following needs:

- An environment of spiritual growth.
- An atmosphere of God's presence.
- A place to belong to a genuine community.
- A family to help meet your needs.
- A place of covering and protection.
- A place for accountability and safety.
- A place for wisdom, direction, and counsel.
- A place to make a difference.
- An opportunity to pour your life into others.
- A safe atmosphere to raise families.
- A place to give of finances, time, and energy.

## The Church God Is Building Today

Have you ever watched the construction process of a massive skyscraper? One day after the next, this monstrous building is being built, immovable and within the sight of everyone. God has called us to partner with Him in building His church. Who you are and where you're going are intricately intertwined in God's greater plan of extending His church. The Church that He is building today is *in* you and *with* you. The following statements regarding the Church apply to you. *You* are the Church!

- The Church is unified (John 17:20–23).

- The Church is victorious (Matt. 16:18–19).
- The Church has authority (Luke 10:19).
- The Church has dominion (Eph. 1:19–23).
- The Church is multicultural and multiethnic (Rev. 5:9).
- The Church is influential (Matt. 16:15–20; Acts 2:47).
- The Church is glorious (Eph. 5:23–32).
- The Church is the fullness of Christ (Eph. 4:11–13).
- The Church is intended for all people (2 Pet. 3:9).

## Your Local Church and Your Purpose

I am both honored and humbled to serve with a great team of leaders that have given themselves to each other and to the cause of Christ for more than thirty years. We have come to realize and fully embrace that so much more can be done to extend God's kingdom if we work together rather than go it alone.

> **SO MUCH MORE CAN BE DONE TO EXTEND GOD'S KINGDOM IF WE WORK TOGETHER RATHER THAN GO IT ALONE.**

It's time for every Christ follower to commit to being a part of the solution and not the problem. Together we can make a difference to strengthen local churches all over the world. You are of definite strength to your pastor and local church; allow them to be strength to you. Your destiny depends on it.

I still recall, as a child, driving with my family through the redwood forest. Those towering trees were so huge, you could actually drive a car through one (and we did). These trees are considered to be the largest natural living things on earth and the tallest trees in the world. Some are more than three hundred feet high and more than 2,500 years old! You'd think that trees so large would have a tremendous root system reaching down hundreds of feet into the earth. The redwoods actually have a very shallow root system, but the key is that they all intertwine.[13] They are locked to each other. Even when the storms come or the winds blow, the redwoods stand strong! Their strength comes by standing together, not alone.

You are on a journey of discovery, making sense of who you are and where you're going. In God's great plan, He desires you to tower like a giant redwood. In His wisdom, He placed in you the perfect mixture of passions, gifts, talents, and personal makeup to allow you to become who you are. That will happen, but only as you give yourself to serving His Church. Your strength comes from standing together, not alone.

# CHAPTER THIRTEEN

# FINDING YOUR PLACE ON THE TEAM

## BECOMING PART OF GOD'S WINNING TEAM

> "In this way we are like the various parts of a
> human body. Each part gets its meaning from the
> body as a whole, not the other way around. The
> body we're talking about is Christ's body of chosen
> people. Each of us finds our meaning and function
> as a part of his body ... So since we find ourselves
> fashioned into all these excellently formed and
> marvelously functioning parts in Christ's body, let's
> just go ahead and be what we were made to be."
>
> —Romans 12:4–6, MSG

I f you didn't know better, you'd think this warehouse was being robbed.
That shuffling sound from the back corner is too deliberate to be a hungry
rat, but still it makes you wonder who's back there. And why? There's
something fishy going on here, and it isn't just the eight-foot-tall stack of
canned tuna boxes. It isn't the pallet of Corn Flakes, the tower of Skippy
peanut butter, or the rows and rows of Hamburger Helper that fill this urban
cavern either; these ten tons of foodstuff staples are quite within context here.
So what is it?

Make your way through this labyrinth, this cornucopia of provision, and
you'll find Joseph Branchflower, a skateboard-retired Generation Xer who's
clad paradoxically in dingy work pants and gleaming, lavishly expensive
Italian shoes (he also moonlights as an Internet shoe merchant). Joseph throws
another family-of-six food box into the back of the church van and begins
assembling another one. Another answered prayer for a family in need.

Joseph has found his purpose. It seems like food ministry is what he was born to do, which is not to underemphasize his sharp business sense—Joseph is a successful and ambitious businessman. In fact, like his gleaming expensive shoes, something about Joseph's professional demeanor is ironic of the warehouse environment where he feels within his element. Assembling these boxes gives him a feeling of great purpose. Why? Because he can identify with the box's varied recipients.

"I grew up in poverty," he explains. "I learned to steal at a young age … it helped me to get what I needed. I remember always being scared; I didn't know if we were going to run out of food or if we'd be able to pay rent or be kicked out of our apartment. My best meals were the free lunches I got at school."

When his parents divorced, his dad took to the streets where he survived by collecting bottles and cans; his mom tried easing her tension by pursuing her newfound spiritual mediums and psychics. "It was a rough time. No food, no money, no dad … and no God."

Like most children, all Joseph ever wanted was to be loved and accepted, to feel secure, like he belonged to something—something real, something significant. As he grew up, he wanted his life to matter for something; he wanted to somehow make a difference. But with no real guidance and support, the "difference" he made was diverted in his teen years to the world of drugs and crime. The detour nearly cost him his life.

"When I turned fifteen, somebody introduced me to marijuana," he says. "I started to experiment with my best friend, and soon we began to use LSD. And then one night, my friend took LSD laced with PCP, and he lost his mind … he ran outside totally naked. He broke through the window of a nearby house and crawled through the jagged glass, which tore his flesh to pieces. Once he was inside the home, he found himself on the floor in a baby's bedroom. All the noise of the shattered glass, my friend screaming and bloody, and the terrified cry of this baby woke up the father, who came racing into the room with his gun. My friend was shot between the eyes that night.

"All this was happening at the time I was walking home, desperately trying to keep my mind in some state of reality. At that point I decided that I just had no idea how to survive; I was unsuccessful at finding any meaning or hope. It was then that I made the conscious decision to remain loaded, to drown my sorrows and pain by living in a constant, stoned stupor. I thought in that place of semiconsciousness I'd be able not to lose any more ground in my sanity, so I found the best solution was suspended reality. I was successful at suspending my life and any purpose for seven years."

And then God showed up! Through an amazing encounter at a local church, Joseph gave his life to Christ and was introduced to a whole new reality. His new church family loved him unconditionally and believed in him for who he was going to become. Joseph found what he had been searching for all along: a place to belong, a place to serve, and a place of significance.

"As soon as I gave my life to Christ, I saw the light of life," he explains. "Just the experience of His love caused me to realize that there was a profound purpose for my life. I was so thrilled to have found this new life; I committed myself to helping others find the same grace that was extended to me. Deep inside I felt that this desire to serve God could—and would—impact this world in a big way. I began searching for ways to prepare myself to accomplish this end."

Joseph has become an integral part of a thriving local church that is committed to reaching its city through providing food and clothing to thousands of hurting people. In large part due to Joseph's contribution, his church has become the single largest distributor of food to families in his entire state. His life experiences and his passion for helping those in need have catapulted him into a very specific place designed by God just for him.[1]

---

## There Are Many Positions to Play

God's wants His Church to be thriving, growing, and victorious. The Bible says, "On this rock I will build my church, and the gates of death will not overcome it" (Matt. 16:8, TNIV). There is no force, no principality, no demon in hell, nor any ruler of the air that will overcome the Church. God's team is a winning team! We will prevail. That doesn't mean we won't face innings where we're down by a few runs, but the Bible assures us that, in the end, we will  win!

This winning team has many positions. In order for any local church to succeed in fulfilling its ultimate calling, the need to mobilize the entire church into places of service is crucial. God's original intent and design are that the entire team be actively involved in serving in ministry. Gone are the days of the pastor doing everything. In fact, those days should have never started in the first place. The Bible makes it pretty clear that those in leadership are gifts to the body of Christ "to equip his people for works of service, so that the body of Christ may be built up" (Eph. 4:12, TNIV). That doesn't mean that the role of pastors and leaders is now deemed insignificant or that they should sit back and have everyone else do the work. On the contrary, God's idea is that everyone participates in building a thriving local church, where no one is left behind and where we all work together to impact our world for Christ.

If this is God's desired blueprint, regardless of the size of your church, hundreds of positions need to be filled in order to pull it off. Without everyone involved, the plan will surely be minimized in its potential.

Recently, I attended a Seattle Mariners baseball game at Safeco Field. I don't know if it's the same at every ballpark in America, but there was one dominant theme from the time you entered the park until the moment you left. Every person in the Mariners organization played a vital role in making the Saturday afternoon game an incredible experience. First there was Sandy, the lady who took our tickets. With a big smile and an enthusiastic voice, she said, "We're glad to have you here; we really hope you enjoy yourself. It should be a great game; you're in for a treat!" She set an expectation in our hearts before we even got through the gates. (I wonder what would happen if our churches treated guests that way?)

Then there was Rafael. He was exuberantly shouting at every passerby to come and indulge in one of his footlong hot dogs. I don't know if, in my entire life, I've ever seen someone so passionate about a half-pound of ground-up pig parts. But contrary to my better judgment, Rafael gladly took my six bucks, and I ingested his 100-percent health-free hot dog.

One of the most memorable events of the day was between the fourth and fifth innings. The groundskeepers were out on the field raking the dirt around the bases, when suddenly music started blasting through the stadium speakers; they all lined up behind second base and performed a dance routine like they were on a Broadway stage. The fans rose to their feet and cheered as if the groundskeepers were the reason we came! The act even made ESPN highlights that evening.

Then there was Edgar Martinez. He never came out to play defensively, but he played an important role as a designated batter, hitting two home runs. I'm sure Edgar didn't complain about not having the chance to play in the field; he knew his responsibility was to knock the ball out of the park, so that's what he did.

In the last inning, Shigetoshi Hasegawa came out and pitched thirteen pitches to clinch the game. It didn't appear that he was bitter about not pitching the other eight innings because he knew his part and played it well. (By the way, he makes a lot of money for those thirteen pitches.)

The day was successful because hundreds of people understood that it takes a lot of people, each one playing their part, serving with passion and excitement, to pull off a successful event. The result was that the entire team participated in winning the game. Imagine if the only ones who showed up to the ballpark that day

**THERE ARE MANY PLACES WHERE YOU COULD SERVE, BUT VERY FEW WHERE YOU SHOULD SERVE.**

were the players. The crowd would be in pandemonium! Who would open the gates? Where would people sit? Who would sell the footlong hot dogs? And who would give directions? Chaos would ensue.

What if only the right-fielder showed up? It doesn't matter that Ichiro Suzuki is one of the best outfielders and highest percentage hitters of all time; there would have been no way to win the game with only one guy in the outfield. Many other players are needed.

So it is with your church. God needs every person to find his or her place on the team and serve well. There are many places where you *could* serve, but very few where you *should* serve. Reserve time in your schedule for the tasks God has created you for. You have a very specific and important role. "God has placed the parts in the body, every one of them, just as he wanted them to be" (1 Cor. 12:18, TNIV). Did you catch that? The text reads "every one of them" and "just as he wanted them to be." God wants each of us to know that it takes the entire body to advance His purposes. Could it be that churches today are struggling to do anything of significance because there aren't enough players in the field, or perhaps because the players aren't in the right position? You be the judge.

## Your Position Is Important to Your Team's Success

We have established that there are many positions needed in order to be successful in fulfilling God's purpose. The next step is to realize that, although there are many possible positions, there is one that fits you best, and that position is incredibly important to the success of your church.

Paul wrote about this important truth using the analogy of the human body.

> I want you to think about how all this makes you more significant, not less. A body isn't just a single part blown up into something huge. It's all the different-but-similar parts arranged and functioning together. If Foot said, "I'm not elegant like Hand, embellished with rings; I guess I don't belong to this body," would that make it so? If Ear said, "I'm not beautiful like Eye, limpid and expressive; I don't deserve a place on the head," would you want to remove it from the body? If the body was all eye, how could it hear? If all ear, how could it smell? As it is, we see that God has carefully placed each part of the body right where he wanted it. (1 Cor. 12:14–18, MSG)

Isn't this refreshing news? Although there are many important parts to God's body, your part is as equally important as all the others. Doesn't this revelation remove any sense of comparison? Doesn't this do something to thwart that feeling of discontentment because you weren't created exactly like your pastor? Paul offered further encouragement: "On the contrary, those parts of the body that seem to be weaker are indispensable" (1 Cor. 12:22, TNIV). You may feel less important, but to God you are most important.

Settle it now: God wants you to be you. "All these are the work of one and the same Spirit, and he distributes them to each one, just as he determines" (1 Cor. 12:11, TNIV). Your specific and unique makeup was specially designed for something only you can do. Remember chapter 4? No one can be you but you. Stop trying to be someone you were never intended to be and begin enjoying who God designed you to be. It is somewhat offensive to God and an embarrassment to yourself to discount His perfect creation.

Each week, I am part of a very important programming meeting that discusses the weekend services in our church. Most people who attend one of our weekend services would have no idea the amount of time, prayer, energy, and preparation that goes into pulling off nine, ninety-minute services in multiple locations. "You just open up the church doors and start singing, right?" Wrong!

There in that meeting, Pastor Frank leads the charge, giving direction and sharing his heart as to how he feels the service should go. The emcees are responsible to guide and direct the entire service, ensuring that an atmosphere of worship is created and that all the details take place in their proper order. The audio-visual guys are responsible to simulcast our campuses together during the message. There needs to be the right image projections on screen for each song and the sermon, brought up at the appropriate time. An individual is responsible for coordinating ushers and door greeters who makes sure the bulletins are handed out, people are loved and greeted, communion elements are prepared, and buckets are passed for the tithes and offerings. Our music director coordinates the song list, transitions, and whatever needs to take place during the worship time.

Whew! Now imagine just one of those people skipping out on a service. What if the audio-visual guys felt that their role was not important? What if, instead of showing up, they decided to go to Starbucks and drink vanilla lattes? The service would be a disaster. But thank God for our home team—James, Alan, and John—who know that what they do is critical to pulling off a great service fifty-two weekends a year.

**NO ONE ELSE CAN BE YOU BUT YOU. STOP TRYING TO BE SOMEONE YOU WERE NEVER INTENDED TO BE AND BEGIN ENJOYING WHO GOD DESIGNED YOU TO BE. IT IS SOMEWHAT OFFENSIVE TO GOD AND AN EMBARRASSMENT TO YOURSELF FOR YOU TO DISCOUNT HIS PERFECT CREATION.**

What if the nursery workers felt their role was insignificant and decided to jump the good ship lollipop? But Jeremy and Debie feel it's crucial to have top-quality love and care for our young, so they and their team devote a great deal of their lives to our children. Be sure to thank your nursery workers often!

What if the custodian decides to stay home to watch football and doesn't open up the facilities? That would be one cold Sunday service. But thank God for David! Not only are the doors opened on time every week, but the coffee is brewing, and he is the first to greet you with a big smile. He loves what he does.

The point is this: Everyone is important! Each role is vital! You are needed! Your pastor needs you, your church needs you, your community needs you! As Paul so adequately said in 1 Corinthians 12:27, "Now all of you together are Christ's body, and each one of you is a separate and necessary part of it" (NLT).

## You Have Been Equipped to Succeed

One of the main comments I hear from people is that they feel inadequate. Even the great leader Moses faced this when God called him to lead Israel.

Moses felt inadequate, but the Lord reminded him that he had everything he needed to fulfill his purpose. "Moses said to the Lord, 'Pardon your servant, Lord. I have never been eloquent, neither in the past nor since you have spoken to your servant. I am slow of speech and tongue.' The Lord said to him, 'Who gave human beings their mouths? Who makes them deaf or mute? Who gives them sight or makes them blind? Is it not I, the Lord? Now go; I will help you speak and will teach you what to say'" (Exod. 4:10–12, TNIV). Who'd have thought that the guy who wrote the first five books of the Bible, who met God on the mountaintop, who parted the Red Sea would be someone who felt inadequate?

Take a moment and reflect on all of the self-discovery exercises you completed while reading chapters 5 through 11. What are you passionate about? Who put those passions in your life? How about your spiritual gifts or talents? Don't you find it fascinating how God divinely orchestrated your entire life with all the intricate parts that have made you who you are?

In one sense, I guess the feeling of being inadequate can be a blessing in disguise, as we do need to totally depend on and trust in God for our strength, not becoming too confident in ourselves. But on the other hand, we must recognize that what God has called us to, He has also equipped us to do and expects us to fulfill. The Bible says, "For we are God's handiwork, created in Christ Jesus to do good works, which God prepared in advance for us to do" (Eph. 2:10, TNIV). We were created, given a purpose, and equipped with everything we need—in advance—to accomplish it.

God has given you everything you need to succeed. He has given you a fresh start on life; you are a new creation! He has given you His Holy Spirit to guide, comfort, direct, and challenge you. He has adorned you with supernatural faith to believe for the impossible. He has built into you God-ordained spiritual gifts, passions, and talents for fulfilling His purposes. He has planted a vision and dream in your heart to give you a future and a hope. He supplies all of your needs.

It is time we stop focusing on our weaknesses and begin focusing on God's strengths. He has already given us the grace we need to accomplish all He asks us to … despite our weaknesses and shortcomings. "Grace has been given as Christ apportioned it" (Eph. 4:7, TNIV).

## God Is Counting on You

As you walk toward the batter's box, you need only to rehearse these thoughts in your mind: "I have the privilege of being a part of God's winning team, the Church. I am important to its success. I am part of the body of Christ! I was planted here for a purpose. I am called to be fruitful." Those who step up are guaranteed to knock the ball out of the park. God promises, "They are like

**IT IS TIME WE STOP FOCUSING ON OUR WEAKNESSES AND BEGIN FOCUSING ON GOD'S STRENGTHS.**

trees planted along the riverbank, bearing fruit each season without fail. Their leaves never wither, and in all they do, they prosper" (Ps. 1:3, NLT).

It all boils down to you; the choice is yours. It is the bottom of the ninth, two outs, bases loaded, and the owner of the team has placed the bat in your hand. The Holy Spirit announces your name to a great cloud of witnesses, and they are cheering you on. Will you step up to the plate? God wants you to consider the same challenge Paul issued to the church at Ephesus: "I urge you to live a life worthy of the calling you have received" (Eph. 4:1, TNIV). The shoe fits. Wear it.

# CHAPTER FOURTEEN

# GIVING IT ALL YOU'VE GOT
## LIVING A LIFE OF PERSEVERANCE
## AND DETERMINATION

"Therefore, since we are surrounded by such a
huge crowd of witnesses to the life of faith, let us
strip off every weight that slows us down, especially
the sin that so easily hinders our progress. And let
us run with endurance the race that God has set
before us. We do this by keeping our eyes on Jesus,
on whom our faith depends from start to finish."

—Hebrews 12:1–2, NLT

I'll never forget my first encounter with Mike Shreve. It was my first
Sunday morning service in a little church on Highway 50 in South Lake
Tahoe. I had just given my life to Christ. So recent had been my life of drugs,
crime, and careless living that my clothes still smelled like smoke. My wife,
two-year-old daughter Heather, and I were in desperate need of direction. It
was a miracle that my marriage had even made it this far. And there he was,
standing by the back door. Something told me he had something to say to
me, but I thought I might be able to avoid him. Like a heat-seeking missile,
Mike locked his radar on me and walked straight toward me.

My heart was pounding. He smiled and said, "Hi, I'm Mike. Welcome." We
shook hands and he wouldn't let go; he just smiled and looked into my eyes
for what seemed like minutes ... maybe it was. By afternoon, I had shared
with Mike my story and accepted an invitation to his house for a Bible study
at six in the morning. I thought to myself, *6 a.m.? You've got to be joking* ... I'd
never even seen that time of day before (unless it was at the tail end of the
night before), let alone for a Bible study! But something convinced me I had
no choice. So I went.

The next morning Mike told me he wanted to invest his life into mine, if only I was willing to meet him halfway. I accepted the challenge, and that summer I found myself, like so many others before me and since, hanging on Mike's suspended words on the mountain trail.

I can still remember one of his first statements that introduced me to the conviction of God: "If He isn't Lord of all, He isn't Lord at all." I knew I was hooked. I always enjoyed a challenge, but this is the one I would savor for the rest of my life.

Over the next fifteen years, Mike played an instrumental role in my life, challenging me to live life to the fullest, to focus solely on God's purpose, and to give it all I had—my money, my thoughts, my resources … and yes, even my life. He taught me how to pray and read my Bible. He showed to me how to be a husband and a father. He taught me how to budget my money and helped me purchase my first house. He invited my family to join his family on vacations, and we went on ministry trips with them to the Philippines. Mike poured his life into us and gave his all for our all.

From firsthand experience, I can say that Mike will go down in the chronicles of history as a give-it-all-you've-got kind of guy. You may never see him on the front of *Charisma* magazine or preaching in coliseums, but I don't think Mike cares and neither does God. Mike has given it all he has, with what he has, and that is all that matters to God. Whether taking young people on wilderness adventures, constructing church buildings, teaching in the local church, or pouring himself into the lives of anyone whom God puts in his path, Mike is one sold-out guy!

Over the years, I've watched him closely, listened attentively, and, to my recollection, cannot remember a single time when this man ever compromised his total dedication to God. Mike Shreve is my friend, my mentor, and my hero.

---

## How About You?

It has been said that what matters most isn't how you start something, but how you finish it. The world is full of people who boldly spew grandiose ideas and have the best intentions to reach new heights, but end up going nowhere. What's missing in their lives? The answer is passionate resolve—a steely determination to accomplish what they have set their heart to do and what God has called them to, and to push through to accomplish their purpose!

Fulfilling your purpose will take everything you've got. It requires great dedication and focus, not just great ideas and intentions. You might have the greatest potential, but without action, your purpose will remain a mere fantasy. Vision to do great things for God without implementation to make them happen is nothing more than a pipe dream. My best advice to make your dreams come true: wake up and face today with greater clarity and determination than ever before. Give it all you've got; make it happen!

The first thirteen chapters of this book have strategically brought you to a place of grappling with your own reality, a crescendo where you have the opportunity to sign on the dotted line and accept the challenge. This is where the rubber meets the road. As my good friend James Buck says, "Some make it happen, others watch it happen, and a few ask, 'What happened?'" If you don't take this chapter to heart, you may be one step closer to looking back at your life and asking, "What happened?"

> **WHAT MATTERS MOST ISN'T HOW YOU START SOMETHING, BUT HOW YOU FINISH IT.**

Becoming who you're supposed to be is all about finding greatness and using it to fill the blanks in your life with purpose. But greatness will only come to those who are willing to give it all they've got. The stage has been set, and now God, the angels, the great cloud of witnesses (Heb. 12:1), and all of creation are standing back waiting to see if you will take your life and its purpose seriously.

## What Are You Giving Now?

Let's begin by asking some questions that may require some real soul-searching. When it comes to devoting your life to Christ, His cause, and His Church, where are you on the spiritual scale? Are you on a rugged path, single-focused on the goal of reaching the next campsite, or are you casually strolling through the valley picking flowers, forgetting that you're on an Ultimate Adventure? Beyond looking at your time and resources (as discussed in chapter 11), what do you dream about? What do you spend your time thinking about? What really excites you? How passionate are you about giving your purpose all you've got?

Many people approach their spiritual destiny with a laissez-faire attitude, casually drifting through life, giving minimal attention to those things that matter most. This isn't something that most of us do intentionally, but we easily become bombarded with the cares and challenges of life. If we aren't careful, we may actually become derailed by life. Its pleasures and challenges (along with a little assistance from the devil) can keep us from ever accomplishing the reason we were created. The promise to make the change tomorrow is always pushed off for another day, creating a numbing effect to the true reality of what matters most ... your purpose! This approach could cost you your

**GREATNESS WILL ONLY COME TO THOSE WHO ARE WILLING TO GIVE IT ALL THEY'VE GOT.**

life! Proverbs 29:18 says, "If people can't see what God is doing, they stumble all over themselves" (MSG). That is why Jesus reminded us, "Steep your life in God-reality, God-initiative, God provisions ... Give your entire attention to what God is doing right now" (Matt. 6:33–34, MSG). Let me emphasize two key points: "your entire attention" and "right now." If you give God your entire focus with every moment you have, He has promised to take care of you and help you figure out the details of life. Your job is to give Him everything.

## How Much Should You Be Giving?
The Bible is pretty clear about just how much of our lives—time, energy, thoughts, and passions—should be directed toward fulfilling our purpose. Some might think merely attending a weekend service is giving enough of themselves to God. Others might see a deeper commitment of attending, serving, and tithing as the acceptable measure of giving. Unfortunately, the idea of compartmentalizing life into "church" and "personal" categories misses the point altogether; God is after our *everything*. The Bible says, "You do not belong to yourself, for God bought you with a high price" (1 Cor. 6:19–20, NLT). Remember Mike's eternal words, "If He isn't Lord of all, He isn't Lord at all." The standard has been set and the requirement is simple: give it all you've got!

There is a repeated theme in Scripture that is worth mentioning—the law of sowing and reaping. Some have identified this prevailing tenet as the law of divine retribution. It's pretty simple … you get out of life what you put into it. The apostle Paul used the analogy of a farmer, telling the church in Corinth, "Remember this—a farmer who plants only a few seeds will get a small crop. But the one who plants generously will get a generous crop. You must each make up your own mind as to how much you should give" (2 Cor. 9:6–7, NLT). Although the context for these verses is the giving of finances, the principle of sowing and reaping applies to every area of your life.

If you want to see a few people's lives changed with Christ's message of redemption and eternal life, then only tell a few people about it. If you want to see God's presence operating occasionally in your day, then only say a few prayers. If you want to live an average life, then just devote an average part of your life to pursuing average greatness.

However, if you want to know and see God's Word in full operation in your everyday life, you must ingest it every day. If you desire for God to speak to you and use you in great exploits, you must spend quality time in prayer listening and being prompt to obey every time He speaks. If you want God to bless your finances beyond measure, give far beyond what is comfortable. And if you want to fulfill your purpose, you have to give it everything you've got. It's the law of divine retribution; God requires all!

You might be asking, but when is enough really enough? Should there ever be time to enjoy life and the relationships with those around me? Of course, but only as long as your life is kingdom-focused. I'm sure if you had spent some time with Jesus on His journeys with the disciples, you would have seen them having a blast. Laughing, playing jokes on each other, just having fun. Jesus is our joy, not our job. Fulfilling our purpose should be something that we want to pursue, having the time of our lives pursuing it. Though it may cost you everything you have, fulfilling your purpose comes with great dividends. It was never intended to be a life of drudgery.

You will end up devoting your time, energy, and life to the things you perceive to bring you the greatest return. Solomon, who had everything he could have possibly wanted, reflected back on his life, looking over the sum of all his mistakes and successes, and made one sweeping, final, poignant statement about life: "Here is my final conclusion: Fear God and obey his commands, for this is the duty of every person. God will judge us for everything we do, including every secret thing, whether good or bad" (Eccles. 12:13–14, NLT).

Although there may be some debate to actual interpretation of this portion of Scripture, humor me for a moment and just consider the possibility of what it might be like some day if you were to stand before the Lord of Hosts and before all of creation for a public viewing of *This Is Your Life*. What a day that cosmic retelling of your personal life journey would be! The fact of the matter is, whether multitudes are viewing the day of reckoning or not, one thing is for sure. Everything we've ever done—the good, bad, and ugly, including our most secret things—will be judged by God according to His Word and His intended purpose for our lives.

I'm reminded of a powerful story of several Chinese Christians who wanted to reach their region with the Gospel of Christ, yet through repeated efforts, received no positive response from the people. They were destitute, living in the forest, scavenging for food to keep them alive. Discouraged, they fasted for a week and prayed for God's guidance. When they gathered to discuss what they should do, each person said they believed God was directing them to stay in the region and wash people's feet.

So for three years they sat on the side of the road with buckets of water, offering to wash the farmers' feet as they were coming and going from the fields. The offer annoyed the farmers, who regularly beat the evangelists and dumped the water on them. But the Christians didn't give up. Finally, one of the farmers let one of the Christians wash his feet, and when he did, the other farmers relented. For three months they washed 1,500 farmers' feet twice a day. And finally, one of the farmers asked, "Why are you doing this?"

Their opportunity to share the Gospel with these farmers came three years and three months after they decided to stay and wash feet. A few weeks later, the Gospel had triumphed in the hearts of the farmers, and they all placed their faith in Jesus Christ, as did another 50,000 residents of the region within two years.[1]

These dedicated Chinese Christians reaped what they sowed! Yes, it cost them a great deal, but the time was worth the effort.

## Steps to Giving Your All

Jesus gave His all, and He requires that we give nothing less than whole-hearted dedication to Him and His purposes. In essence, we need to be like a postage stamp, stuck in our place until we arrive at our final destination.

Giving it all you've got isn't as confusing as it may sound. On the contrary, it is very simple. It isn't necessarily easy, but it is definitely simple. The writer of the book of Hebrews illustrated three simple steps to sensibly giving it all we've got. "Therefore, since we are surrounded by such a huge crowd of witnesses to the life of faith, let us strip off every weight that slows us down, especially the sin that so easily hinders our progress. And let us run with endurance the race that God has set before us. We do this by keeping our eyes on Jesus, on whom our faith depends from start to finish" (Heb. 12:1–2, NLT).

**Step One: Remove anything that slows you down.**
The very first thing that is required is to remove anything in our lives that would hinder our forward motion. "Let us strip off" literally means laying off old clothes, in preparation for the race.[2] During the first century, runners in the coliseum races would tear off their outer clothing and robes so that only minimal clothing would be left. Some commentaries say they ran nearly naked. Now, obviously they weren't "streakers," but their objective was to remove anything that might slow them down.

Hebrews 12 goes on to describe the two areas that we should consider: "every weight" and "the sin that so easily hinders our progress."

*"Every weight"*: The emphasis here is on added pressure or weight that might distract your focus and energies from the finish line. Sometimes things become part of your thoughts, emotions, and actions that may not necessarily be sin, but are weights that cloud your ability to be single-focused. These may be past hurts or experiences that cause you to move forward with reservation or reluctance. It might be that you have feelings of insecurity or inadequacy that paint a distorted picture in your mind of who you really are. These are things that pull you down when you should be ascending upward, and pull you back when you should be pressing forward; these weights make kingdom duty harder and heavier than it was intended to be.

Whatever it might be, the challenge is to remove all that might obstruct progress in an effort to win the crown of life. Choose to remove it now.

*"Remove any sin that so easily hinders your progress"*: There isn't one person alive that is pardoned from this. We all have varying degrees of sin, but despite its frequency, sin is the number-one contributor to slowing you down from fulfilling your purpose.

Ted Haggard defines sin as "missing God's best plan for your life."[3] In his book, *Foolish No More*, he says, "Sin will take you farther than you want to go, keep you longer than you want to stay, and cost you more than you want to pay … Don't sin! Sin messes us up. Because sin is living contrary to God's plan for our lives, it is forfeiting the destiny He has for us. It's going in a direction we were not designed to go. It just doesn't work as it should … Sin is rejecting God and choosing another lord that offers a shallow kind of gratification that is only temporary … A lifetime of good living can be destroyed by ten minutes of sin."[4]

Is there any sin in your life that is slowing your progress in God? Don't procrastinate; deal with it. Make the choice now to leave it behind you. Removing sin from your life is far more important than finishing this chapter. Take a moment and pray about it … right now!

**Step Two: Run the race with everything you've got!**
The writer of Hebrews compared our lives to a race, not a walk through the park. A race speaks of urgency! How you finish determines your reward—or lack thereof. The race analogy also reflects the necessary time spent in training and preparation. It hints at being in the best possible shape in order to finish the great things God has for us. Paul, writing to the Corinthians, drove home this point: "Run in such a way as to get the prize. Everyone who competes in the games goes into strict training. They do it to get a crown that will not last; but we do it to get a crown that will last forever. Therefore I do not run like someone running aimlessly; I do not fight like a boxer beating the air. No, I strike a blow to my body and make it my slave so that after I have preached to others, I myself will not be disqualified for the prize" (1 Cor. 9:24–27, TNIV).

The race of life is active, not passive. It is a race with specific course requirements. It isn't a sprint but a marathon. It isn't in a lit stadium, but winds through the streets of real life. God desires that we run with endurance, perseverance, and passion. He wants us focused on the goal. William Booth, one of my heroes of the faith, had **THE RACE OF LIFE IS ACTIVE,** the proper perspective on running **NOT PASSIVE.** with endurance and was able to lead more than 250,000 people to Christ in just a few years through the ministry he started called the Salvation Army. He said, "There have been men with greater brains than I, even with greater opportunities, but from the day I got the poor of London on my heart and caught a vision of what Jesus Christ could do with me and them, on that day I made up my mind that God should have all of William Booth there was. And if there is anything of power in the Salvation Army, it is because God has had all the adoration of my heart, all the power of my will, and all the influence of my life."[5]

Nothing in this world can take the place of persistence. Talent cannot compete with it; noth-

**RUNNING THE RACE WELL IS DIRECTLY TIED TO OUR ABILITY TO KEEP OUR MOTIVES PURE AND OUR PURPOSE CLEAR.**

ing is more common than unsuccessful men with talent. Genius cannot figure it out; unrewarded genius is almost a proverb. Education cannot earn it; the world is full of educated derelicts. Persistence and determination are key to being able to face all that life throws at you and still be able to finish strong.

**Step Three: Focus on Jesus.**
The final step (which is the most important, yet most neglected) is masterfully articulated in Hebrews, "We do this by keeping our eyes on Jesus, on whom our faith depends from start to finish" (12:2, NLT). Running the race well is directly tied to our ability to keep our motives pure and our purpose clear. Our focus and our purpose reside in Jesus, our Lord and Savior.

You'd be hard-pressed to find anyone in the Bible—or *ever* for that matter— who has done anything great for God without a completely dedicated life of focusing on Him. He is our source of strength, our high tower, our ever-present help in time of need. He is our comfort, our peace, and our joy. He is our Savior and Lord. He is our all in all. He is the reason we exist. Therefore our purpose must be in Him and for Him. Every waking moment should be dedicated to Him and His purposes as stated in Colossians 3:23: "Whatever you do, work at it with all your heart, as working for the Lord" (TNIV). Every thought should be subject to His Word and purposes, and all others should be thrown out. We are instructed to "demolish arguments and every pretension that sets itself up against the knowledge of God, and we take captive every thought to make it obedient to Christ" (2 Cor. 10:5–6, TNIV).

It is the combination of these three great truths—removing anything that slows you down, running the race with everything you've got, and focusing on Jesus—that will get you moving toward fulfilling the purposes of God.

## Finishing Strong

Living every day with a determined passion toward our purpose may be a challenge, but it's not unreachable. This perseverance needs to become more of a daily habit in our lives than a good intention. Ultimately, if we are able to make this pursuit our life-focus, we are well on our way to making sense of who we are and where we are going.

I am saddened by the culture in which we live that has set up the idea that we work our entire lives to relax at the finish line. I am all for slowing down as I get older, as I know I won't be able to live at the pace in which I currently operate, but I don't want to fill my mind for the next twenty years with the thought that I am simply going to roll up the carpet, pack up my bags, and just relax and "take thine ease." Please don't take this as a slam against retirement. All I'm saying is that regardless of the season of our life, our everyday focus needs to be one of purpose.

The Bible is full of people who did great things for God. Even of the three hundred leaders mentioned, more than two-thirds of them didn't finish well. I believe these examples have been left for us to see that their lives never really reached their true potential. Imagine if Achan wouldn't have gotten greedy and hid some articles under his tent (Josh. 7). What if Absalom didn't rebel against his father, King David (2 Sam. 15–17)? Would he have been in line for a great inheritance? How about Samson and all of his strength, who gave in at the last minute to a seductive woman who ultimately short-circuited his life (Judg. 16)? Then there's Judas, who was one of the twelve chosen disciples who sold out his destiny for thirty pieces of silver (Matt. 26:14–16). Ananias and Sapphira went the way of the flesh as well, choosing a lie over the truth (Acts 5:1–11).

**LIVING EVERY DAY WITH A DETERMINED PASSION TOWARD OUR PURPOSE MAY BE A CHALLENGE, BUT IT'S NOT UNREACHABLE.**

Each of these people had the same opportunity that you and I have. The difference is that it's too late for them to make it right. You, my friend, have time right now. Will you choose to give yourself to your purpose and strive for excellence?

Let us savor the words of Paul, who finished strong and finished well. Here's a man of God, imprisoned for his faith, penning some of his final thoughts. It would seem natural to be discouraged; his life is nearly over, no one is coming to visit him in jail, waves of loneliness overtake him. But Paul had nothing to regret. He had given everything he had to fulfill his purpose. He traveled to different nations preaching the Gospel. He assisted in planting local churches. He wrote two-thirds of the New Testament. As he writes his parting thoughts to his young disciple, Timothy, he proudly says, "I have fought the good fight, I have finished the race, I have kept the faith. Now there is in store for me the crown of righteousness, which the Lord, the righteous Judge, will award to me on that day—and not only to me, but also to all who have longed for his appearing" (2 Tim. 4:7–8, TNIV).

What a powerful way to end one's life! Paul finished strong. He has received his great reward. He gave it all he had. He heard those long-awaited words of his Savior: "Well done." In closing, I want you to catch those last few words he said, "Not only to me, but also to all who have longed for his appearing." The way I read it, he was speaking to you …. and to me. The reward Paul received is one that potentially awaits us. Will you run the race with eagerness? Will you give it all you've got?

I am forever grateful for the example set for me by Leonard and Rosella Fox. This incredible couple devoted their lives to God. Rosella, who recently went home to be with the Lord, was preaching and prophesying until that last days of her eighty-plus years on earth. Leonard, although fragile, is still determined to travel the globe sharing the good news of Jesus Christ. Lord, help us to burn for You as long as we have breath.

CHAPTER FIFTEEN

# THE DAY AFTER
## LEAVING A LEGACY OF PURPOSE

"You have heard me teach many things that have
been confirmed by many reliable witnesses. Teach
these great truths to trustworthy people who are
able to pass them on to others."

—2 Timothy 2:2, NLT

It wasn't an easy life, and this was no easy death either ... pulmonary fibrosis made sure of that. Lung tissue hardens under this cruelly debilitating bout, wreaking either drawn-out suffocation or a shutting-down of the heart. But the man in the bed lay smiling.

"Bill, why would God let you suffer like this?" his wife, Vonette, asked.

"I am not suffering; Jesus suffered," the inexhaustible crusader answered. "Here I am at home in beautiful surroundings with people who love me, and I am not suffering."[1]

For months, Dr. Bill Bright had been preparing for the end. Doctors issued the grim prognosis that it would come and that it wouldn't be easy; he would suffocate, he would choke, he would panic, it would be painful. Unfazed, Bill went to work. If the end was near, he had lots to do. He needed to tie up the details of the eighty different projects he had under way, including plans to train five million lay pastors to start five million churches around the world and the International Leadership University, housed in the Empire State Building, which aims to equip tens of millions of students with a biblical worldview.[2] His final project was the book he co-authored with his wife, titled *The Journey Home*, wrapping up a lifetime of triumphs tracking the purposes of God throughout the world for generations to come.

But long before illness gripped his body, an all-consuming determination to reach the world with the message of Christ gripped Bill's soul. In 1951 Bill and Vonette founded Campus Crusade for Christ, a ministry establishing itself on forty college campuses in the United States and two other countries within its first ten years. Bill was determined to reach every college campus in the world for Christ.

In the 1960s, Campus Crusade for Christ conducted a survey on Christianity to college students across the nation. When it was complete, staff member Ney Bailey presented the sobering results to Bill: students flatly didn't know how to become a Christian. Bill sifted slowly through the results, looking at survey after survey, repeating to himself, "They don't know how … they don't know how." Finally, he put down the surveys and sobbed. Such deep compassion for people who live life fending for themselves without Christ, and the all-consuming passion to know God more himself, unleashed Bill's personal mandate: for every person in the world to have an opportunity to know the Savior whom he loved so much.

Bill's humble beginnings, coupled with his unquenchable desire to see all people presented with the Gospel, cultivated a lifestyle of building God's kingdom … one day at a time, one person at a time, one opportunity at a time. Under Bill's direction, Campus Crusade has seen great accomplishments over the years. The organization has 25,000 full-time staff and more than 553,000 volunteers in 196 countries. The organization's *Jesus* film has been translated into more than seven hundred languages—seen by 5.4 billion people, the most widely viewed film ever produced—and they have distributed more than 2.5 billion copies of their Gospel booklet, *Four Spiritual Laws*.

These accomplishments came through a man who understood purpose and believed that through God, all things are possible. His entire life and ministry were paved with the idea of taking biblical truths and pouring them into the lives of others.

In the early 1990s, Bill began sensing the modern Church's need to put more emphasis on prayer and fasting. He led the way by embarking on a forty-day fast, asking God to raise up one million people to follow in his footsteps, the results of which far exceeded his expectations as millions of leaders and Christians joined together in fasting and prayer. In 1996, he received the prestigious Templeton Prize for Progress Toward Research or Discoveries about Spiritual

Realities, worth more than $1 million. He donated all of his prize money to causes promoting the spiritual benefits of fasting and prayer.[3]

At the last session of the June 2002 Southern Baptist Convention in Saint Louis, Bill shared, "To surrender yourself totally, irrevocably, without reservation to the living Christ is the greatest privilege man can know ... I am eighty years old and just beginning to really understand, though I've preached it for many years, the importance of being dead to Bill Bright. Bill Bright has no rights in my life. Christ has purchased me; I belong to Him. And if I refuse to walk in the light as He is in the light, I am the loser."[4]

This was his life. And people noticed. In his last days, word spread quickly about Bill's condition. About a month before his death, he received a call from President George W. Bush. "It was a nice call, and I was honored," Bill said, "but when you're preparing to meet who I'm about to meet, even a call from the president fades in comparison."[5]

In the end, Bill lay joyful in the bed, holding his wife's hand and surrounded by his family who, at his request, sang songs of victory. This is what really mattered. His labored breathing had dropped to about four breaths a minute when Vonette leaned in and whispered into his ear, "Honey, I want you to go be with Jesus." His next breath was in glory.

Radio talk show host Mike Ebert said of Bill, "He had amazing perspective because he knew his purpose and he never wavered from it. It's a great lesson for all of us about the way we need to live our lives. We need to always be living with the end in mind—this life here is not going to last forever."[6]

In a videotaped message he prepared before his death, Bill Bright shared, "For you who know Jesus Christ personally, I have a word for you: Do not settle for mediocrity. You are a child of the God of the universe. Surrender to Him. Become His slave. I can assure you, after more than fifty years of experience, there is no greater adventure than following Him. He cares for you. Take Him at His Word ... What I have believed by faith I am now experiencing in reality. I now see my Savior with my own eyes and I hear him with my own ears as I worship Him in a way I have never understood. This is a good day for me. I pray it will be a good one for you. God bless each of you."[7]

## How Will You Be Remembered the Day After?

If your body, ravaged and debilitated, gave up your spirit, would there be anything that remains of your efforts on earth? Could you be accurately portrayed by simple observation of your fruit? How many would stand at your memorial service and attribute their spiritual condition to the time and effort you poured into them? Have you laid a spiritual foundation for ministry that will endure long after your body fades away? Will history reflect your private prayer?

Last week in church my son, Kyle, was sitting next to me during worship. He was using a twisted paper clip to pick out pebbles from the tread of his shoe, and the Holy Spirit quickly reminded me of this book. I paused and looked around to see the spiritual posture of those surrounding me. Who was hungry? Who was bored? What was the spiritual climate of the service?

One row behind me stood a young blond-haired woman with both hands stretched out like she was grasping desperately for a life preserver, a river of mascara streaming down both cheeks. Something told me she had business to deal with God about.

Looking back to Kyle, with the paper clip now lodged in his mouth, it occurred to me how many lives have been left fallow while others make the most of every moment. You can be sure the next time I see this woman, I'll encourage her to continue pursuing God.

**OUR GENERATION CANNOT BE HELD RESPONSIBLE FOR WHAT PAST GENERATIONS HAVE ACCOMPLISHED OR NEGLECTED, BUT WE WILL BE HELD ACCOUNTABLE WITH WHAT WE DO TODAY AND IN THE GENERATIONS TO COME.**

I came to the realization that, in the end, when we look back over our lives, whatever we behold is completely of our own making. Finding your purpose and getting involved isn't enough. Getting involved and even giving it all you've got isn't enough. We have to realize the history with which we've been entrusted. So many still need to hear the good news, both during and after our lifetime. Our generation cannot be held responsible for what past generations have accomplished or neglected, but we will be held accountable with what we do today and in the generations to come.

This is why Jesus was so bent on pounding the "reproduction gene" into the lives of His people. He knew how critical it would be for every believer to leave a legacy long after they were gone. In His great discourse about being on the vine (John 15), Jesus shared some of His most intimate thoughts regarding life's purpose and the importance of using your purpose to extend His kingdom through the lives of others. He said, "You did not choose me, but I chose you and appointed you so that you might go and bear fruit—fruit that will last" (John 15:16, TNIV). The entire chapter addresses the point that Christians are called to be fruitful, to find our purpose and fulfill it. Jesus made it clear that a tree (your life) is meant to be fruitful, bearing good fruit. In addition, He warned His disciples that non-fruit-bearing trees would be cut off. But His final point was that we should bear fruit "that will last." It is vital that we understand that whatever Jesus invests into us, we are meant to pass on to others.

In another account, Jesus shared with many along the seashore the parable of the sower and the seed.

> Then he told them many things in parables, saying: "A farmer went out to sow his seed. As he was scattering the seed, some fell along the path, and the birds came and ate it up. Some fell on rocky places, where it did not have much soil. It sprang up quickly, because the soil was shallow. But when the sun came up, the plants were scorched, and they withered because they had no root. Other seed fell among thorns, which grew up and choked the plants. Still other seed fell on good soil, where it produced a crop—a hundred, sixty or thirty times what was sown. Whoever has ears, let them hear." (Matt. 13:3–9, TNIV)

Keep in mind, God is the farmer, the seed is the Gospel, and where the seed falls represents both a person's receptivity and their response to investing their lives into God's purposes. The phrase you must get is, "Still other seed fell on good soil, where it produced a crop—a hundred, sixty or thirty times what was sown. Whoever has ears, let them hear." Jesus wanted us to know that the seed that has been placed in our lives should be reproduced, even one hundred fold! He has given us the dare of a lifetime. Are you game?

Our purpose was given to us for the sake of others, not ourselves. The future of the kingdom is dependent upon His followers today. That includes you. You have a purpose, one worth reproducing even a hundred times over. If you have an ear to hear, we can continue.

## Leaving a Legacy: Multiplying the Purposes of God in Your Life

William Seymour, the man used by God during the Azusa Street Revival at the beginning of the twentieth century, would enter a room graced with the tangible presence of God, walk over to the corner, and put a box over the top of his head, waiting on God to do the rest.[8] He categorically refused to take any credit for what was going on in these historic meetings, and in fact he didn't want anyone to look at him as if he had anything to do with it. Here is a man who understood that the legacy must continue but his name should remain insignificant.

One of my favorite authors, Robert E. Coleman, says, "One must decide where he wants his ministry to count—in the momentary applause of popular recognition or in the reproduction of his life in a few chosen men who will carry on his work after he has gone. Really it is a question of which generation we are living for."[9] With this being our motivation and focus, let's look at five steps we can practically take to apply these reproduction principles to fulfilling our purpose.

### Step One: Build Deliberately

People who have accomplished great things for God understand that the kingdom of God is a forward-advancing kingdom, one that is active and not passive. Your ability to reproduce yourself will be determined greatly on whether you are active or passive in pursuing this call on your life.

Here are some simple tips you can take to start the process of building deliberately:

- *Start serving now.* Decide to get actively involved in putting your purpose to work. Serve faithfully and consistently in your local church.

- *Develop yourself.* Be aggressive in developing and maturing your passions, spiritual gifts, and talents.

- *Look for others to serve alongside of you.* Ask God to direct others to you who can become your disciples.

• *Develop relationships.* Look for ways to build and strengthen lasting friendships with these individuals, both inside and outside of your serving or ministry areas. They may become your lifelong friends!

• *Become a mentor to them.* Allow them access to your life. Give them permission to follow you and watch how you live your life, not just how you do ministry. Mentor them in all areas of their lives.

• *Teach them biblical truths and values.* Let your time together have some biblical focus and content. Use real-life applications as a way to illustrate biblical truths and values.

• *Give them opportunity to experience ministry.* The best way to learn is to do! Jesus followed this principle with His disciples. His method of reproduction went like this, "I do, you watch. I do, you listen. I do, you help. You do, I help. You do, I watch ... You do, I'm gone."

• *Be an example at all times.* People will always do more of what they see than what they are told. Paul made this pretty clear in 1 Corinthians 11:1. He said, "Imitate me, just as I also imitate Christ" (NKJV). Live your life in a way that is honorable to God's Word, and you will reproduce likewise.

## Step Two: Build One Day at a Time

Once we've decided to build deliberately, we must move forward realistically. Rome wasn't built in a day, and your life won't be either. Life is a process, and as you get older, you realize more that the *process* becomes the goal, even more than the goal itself! God desires that you focus on the moment and that you don't lose sight of the now.

I have also learned that great people are built one day at a time, one conversation at a time, one prayer at a time, one experience at a time. Don't be in a hurry for what God has for you tomorrow, because you might miss what He has in store for you today.

This also applies to those whom we are raising up. Let God be the one who brings the increase, while you set your heart on building them up daily and consistently. You will want to make sure they have a sure foundation, one that can withstand the storms and pressures of life. This comes through making sure each brick of their foundation is properly and securely placed in its perfect place and time.

D onna Lasit is an incredibly gifted musician, songwriter, worship leader, mother of three children, and wife of a youth pastor. Donna deliberately pours into others, investing her life to influence a generation of worship leaders and musicians that will bring the presence of God into the lives of Christians across the globe.

For her, it isn't enough that we experience the presence of God now, but that there are others trained to do likewise tomorrow. It is amazing to see the relationships she has forged with young worship leaders and musicians, bringing them into her life and home. She meets with a group of people on Thursday evenings, as well as a smaller group on Saturday mornings, challenging them to live holy lives above reproach.

"Jesus tells us that if we seek Him first and all of His righteous, all the other things in life will work out according to His plan," she says. "I've found it to be true. If I lose my life in His purpose and seemingly lose my dreams, I turn around and find that He is building my life better than I ever could. Every time I lay something down, something greater is there in its place. As I lose my life, I find it! I am more fulfilled now than ever." Her legacy has begun.[10]

### Step Three: Build One Person at a Time

Not only do we need to build deliberately one day at a time, but we also need to focus on one person at a time. This doesn't mean that you can't have multiple mentoring relationships, but it does mean that you need to make sure not to overextend yourself. Doing so renders you useless to any of them.

Jesus spent more time with twelve men than with anyone else. Out of those twelve He was very close with three: Peter, James, and John. Jesus understood that relationships take time, and He was willing to get away from the multitudes and the pressures of life to spend time with the few.

Over the years, God has placed some very special people in my life. These young men have grown to become great leaders in their respective areas of ministry. Alex and I have known each other for almost twenty years. Our relationship started when he was in junior high and I was his youth pastor. There was something about this young man that drew me to him and him to me. For many years I invested my life into him, even taking him on ministry trips. Our relationship today is as strong as ever. The same could be said for Paul, Mike, and Anthony, to name a few. Each of these great young men still holds a very close place in my heart. Throughout the years God has given me certain seasons when I was able to personally invest my life into theirs, and I am as grateful to them as they have told me they are to me.

> **GREAT PEOPLE ARE BUILT ONE DAY AT A TIME, ONE CONVERSATION AT A TIME, ONE PRAYER AT A TIME, ONE EXPERIENCE AT A TIME. DON'T BE IN A HURRY FOR WHAT GOD HAS FOR YOU TOMORROW, BECAUSE YOU MIGHT MISS WHAT HE HAS IN STORE FOR YOU TODAY.**

### Step Four: Build Beyond Yourself

As you make your contribution into others' lives, you must be willing to let them excel beyond your own life. It's a good thing to have ability, but it's a *great* thing to discover the ability of others! There might be the chance that God will use one of those whom you disciple to accomplish far more than you ever will. Someone had to disciple Bill Bright.

One of my favorite heroes in the Bible is Barnabas. Here's a man who was used mightily by God in shaping the life and ministry of the apostle Paul. Paul is the one who gets all the credit for planting the churches and for writing two-thirds of the New Testament, but it was Barnabas who played an instrumental role in shaping Paul.

Scripture tells us that Barnabas went to Tarsus after Saul (who later becomes Paul) and brought him back to the church in Antioch. I wonder what would have happened if Barnabas didn't go. The two ministered together there for a year or so, and in those early years it appears that Barnabas was leading Paul.

In Acts 11–13, there are four accounts where Scripture reads "Barnabas and Saul" (Acts 11:30, 12:25, 13:2, 13:7). It's interesting, then, to note that from Acts 14 on, the reference changes to "Paul and Barnabas" (Acts 13:43, 46, 50). Paul's ministry had matured so much that Barnabas was no longer leading Paul, but vice versa. Barnabas was successful because Paul had become successful. He had reproduced himself and allowed his disciple to far exceed him. We must be willing to do the same.

### Step Five: Build with the End in Mind

A day will come when we will all stand before our Maker. Not only will we be judged by what we do (or don't do), but we will also be rewarded for the fruit we have produced. Your purpose will never be complete without having spiritual grandchildren.

Your goal must never be to just produce people who are active, healthy Christians, but to produce active, healthy, *reproducing* Christians. The process of discipleship and growth will never be complete until the one that you are discipling has begun discipling others, who in turn do likewise. Barnabas mentored Paul, who mentored Timothy. In 2 Timothy 2:2, Paul wrote, "And the things you have heard me say in the presence of many witnesses entrust to reliable people who will also be qualified to teach others" (TNIV). If you look closely, you can see a four-generation reproduction mentioned. Paul mentored Timothy, who in turn was instructed to find reliable men and teach them, and they were to teach others. In essence, Paul was saying, "Timothy, work to produce spiritual great-great grandchildren!"

This four-generation reproduction principle is also found in Ephesians 4:11–12: "So Christ himself gave the apostles, the prophets, the evangelists, the pastors and teachers, to equip his people for works of service, so that the body of Christ may be built up" (TNIV). Reproduce yourself in others and produce spiritual grandchildren. Leave a legacy!

---

Once there was a Yugoslavian woman named Agnes who was highly successful in this process. At age twelve, while praying she felt God called her to give her life to the service of her neighbors. She had no way of knowing that her neighbors would someday be the poorest in the world. As a young lady she traveled to Ireland to begin her education to become a teacher, where she learned about the immense disease and poverty that paralyzed the country of India. Gripped with compassion for these people, she decided to go to India and teach.

She arrived in Calcutta and began teaching history and geography. During those first few years, she found herself taking frequent trips into the most destitute areas of the city, seeing firsthand the plight of those living in heaps of garbage and human waste. Though smallpox, dysentery, and tuberculosis were rampant and there was little medicine to help the dying, she began to see that her purpose in life was to help those who couldn't help themselves. This included raising up people and resources to meet the tremendous need.

In 1948, she received approval as a lone crusader to open a school for the poor, while choosing to move into the area and live among the poor herself. Lacking money and support, her first classroom was an outside area, her first chalkboard the dirt on the ground.

She continued to appeal for assistance and eventually received her first donation, which helped her to build her first real classroom and gather a few medical supplies. Her dedication and passion to stick with the poor in Calcutta gave her a reputation beyond the slums, all the way to the Vatican.

In 1950 the pope granted her permission to begin her own religious order, The Missionaries of Charity. Their motto was, "Whole-hearted and free service to the poorest of the poor, and be positive; a cheerful giver is a great giver." On one occasion, the pope gave her his white Lincoln Continental. She raffled it off for five times its value, raising more than $100,000 for the care of lepers.

As her order grew, she recruited volunteers to assist her in reaching the poor people of India. She raised funds to establish homes for orphans and safe havens for the dying. She quickly became an icon of unconditional love and compassion. While others ran away from the three million contagious and leprous people of India, Agnes ran toward them.

In 1952 the first Home for the Dying was opened in space made available by the city of Calcutta. Over the years, the Missionaries of Charity grew from a dozen volunteers to literally thousands serving the "poorest of the poor" in 450 centers around the world. Agnes created many homes for the dying and unwanted from Calcutta to New York to Albania. She was one of the pioneers of establishing homes for AIDS victims.

When asked about her passion to help the helpless and dying, she said, "The greatest disease today is not leprosy, cancer, or tuberculosis, but the feeling of being unwanted, uncared for, and deserted by everyone." Hopelessness and loneliness were killing millions, and she was the first to notice.

In 1979, Agnes received the Nobel Peace Prize and convinced the committee to cancel the award banquet on her behalf and use the money to feed four hundred poor children for a year.

Despite years of strenuous and dangerous work, Agnes refused to slow down. "I have never said no to Jesus or someone in need, so I am not going to start saying no now!"

**"I HAVE NEVER SAID NO TO JESUS OR SOMEONE IN NEED, SO I AM NOT GOING TO START SAYING NO NOW!"**
—MOTHER TERESA

She died in 1997, and has become an icon of faith and love. She walked with prime ministers and presidents, kings and queens in order to focus the world's attention on the poor. But she never let fame be her focus, to overshadow her burden to fulfill what God called her to do. Agnes, who later became known as Mother Teresa, shared these final words, "Charity begins today. Today somebody is suffering. Today somebody is in the street. Today somebody is hungry. Do not wait for tomorrow."[11]

Today, her efforts and life have been passed on to countless millions. Her legacy goes on. How amazing to see how a solitary woman, fully devoted to God and to His purposes, could accomplish such extraordinary exploits. But to God, it might just be what is expected.

---

You'll never know all that you can accomplish until you give God your all, and give it to others. Mother Teresa did. Bill Bright did. The apostle Paul did. How about you?

## Living for the Day After

Not long ago, I ventured under my house to retrieve some camping gear for a family outing. We have a dirt-floor basement, so the experience wasn't one I much looked forward to. I don't get down there often. To the left of the gear was a stack of boxes that had been there since the day we moved in nine years ago. I thought to myself, "I should throw these boxes out; if I haven't needed them in nine years, chances are I won't ever need them." But my curiosity won out, and I decided to take a peek inside. I opened up the box on top, shuffling through the contents—various papers and office hodgepodge of the type I usually throw away without a second thought—and over the next thirty minutes I finally made my way to the bottom box.

Lo and behold, at the very bottom of this bottom box was a special set of personal notes I had written to God years earlier at a time in my life when I had more questions than answers, but obeyed the clear and enduring voice of God because it was the only thing in my life that was certain. The priceless stack of papers was earnestly held together by a solitary paper clip.

I paused for a moment looking at that stack of treasured notes with the paper clip still attached, reflecting on the front page's intimate words. There I sat on the dirt floor under the basement light, reading the erstwhile sentiments of a man in search of his purpose when my attention was caught by this simple little paper clip, holding these important notes together. I couldn't escape the metaphor. For more than nine years, this faithful little tool had been fulfilling its purpose ... in my basement ... at the very bottom of the very bottom box. Whether anyone would ever see it or not was inconsequential; it was simply fulfilling its intended purpose.

The day will come when God will open the box to your life and delve through its contents. Hopefully when He does, He will find that you lived a deliberate life of purpose, always chasing down the things He had for you, always striving to become who you were meant to be since before time. Hopefully.

From here forward, the rest is up to you. What you do with what you've received will determine where you go in the future. God has done His part, now you must do yours. Now that you understand who you are and where you are going ... go do it!

# PART
# FOUR
## IDENTITY CRISIS RESOLVED

# DEFINING YOUR PASSIONS

## Discovering How Your Passions Are Expressed

The following list is comprised of seventeen passion expressions and their definitions. Please read through the list in its entirety and select the three that you enjoy most. Place these three selections in the blanks at the end of the list:

**Caring**—I really enjoy assisting those who are hurting or in need. There's nothing better than seeing a smile on the face of someone touched by a thoughtful deed.

**Completing**—It's not how you start that matters but how you finish. I love to work through the details to ensure that the task is completed thoroughly.

**Creating**—I enjoy creating materials and systems that don't already exist as well as working on new and innovative ways to convey concepts visually or audibly.

**Designing**—I love to work with technology or materials to produce better ways of communicating.

**Gathering**—Pulling together a team of people or resources to accomplish a task or meet a need is something I love giving my time to.

**Hospitality**—I like to use my home as a place to entertain others, and I enjoy being a part of a team that cooks, serves, or caters for others.

**Intercession**—I love to pray for extended periods of time and sense the Holy Spirit directs me toward specific areas to pray. People consider me to be an intercessor.

**Leading or Overseeing**—I love to lead the charge. I prefer to be directing what's going on, rather than following. Helping others to see the big picture and then working together with them to accomplish the task is something I love to do.

**Maintaining**—I enjoy working with well-established programs and helping to further their success.

**Motivating**—I love to inspire others to do their very best. I love the challenge of helping people see the value and benefits of investing their time, talents, and resources.

**Overcoming**—It's doesn't matter how high the mountain or how long it's going to take—I'm going to get there. I love challenges, and I find a real thrill in figuring out ways to persevere and get the result.

**Perfecting**—I'm always looking for ways to improve things that already exist. Being at and performing to the highest level of excellence is important to me.

**Performing**—Lights, camera, action. I love to be in front of people and help them understand and enjoy a message through creative communication such as drama, music, and the arts.

**Pioneering**—I love to take risks. The idea of trying something new pushes my button.

**Repairing**—If it's broken … I can fix it. I love to tinker with things and get them back to working order.

**Sharing or Giving**—I love to use my resources—time, energy, and money—to make sure others' needs are taken care of.

**Strategizing**—Contemplating all the options and figuring out the best path to get the desired result is something I enjoy.


My top three passion expressions are:

1. _____

2. _____

3. _____

## Discovering the People You're Passionate About

The following list is comprised of thirty-five different categories of people. Please read through the list in its entirety and select the top three groups that you enjoy working with. Place these three selections in the blanks at the end of the list:

| | | |
|---|---|---|
| Infants | Single Parents | Homeless |
| Preschoolers | Divorced | Unemployed |
| Kindergartners | Widowed | Business People |
| Elementary | Senior Citizens | Military |
| Junior High | Emergency Services | Politicians |
| High School | Hospitalized | Prisoners |
| College | Mentally Challenged | Addictions: _____ |
| Young Adults | Handicapped | Ethnic Groups: _____ |
| Singles | Deaf | Athletes: _____ |
| Young Marrieds | Blind | New Believers |
| Young Families | Rich | Spiritual Seekers |
| Married Couples | Poor | |

_____ Other: _____

My top three people passions are:

1. _____

2. _____

3. _____

## Discovering the Issues You're Passionate About

The following list identifies twenty-nine different areas of interest. These can be identified as issues of passion. Please read through the list in its entirety and select the top three issues or causes that you feel strongly about. Place these three selections in the blanks at the end of the list:

The issues or causes I feel strongly about are:

| | | |
|---|---|---|
| Abortion | Education | Mental Health |
| Abuse | Environment | Mentoring |
| Addictions | Family | Politics |
| Adoption | Finances | Poverty |
| AIDS | Health | Racism |
| Business | Homosexuality | Reaching the Lost |
| Childcare | Hunger | Social Concerns |
| Church | Injustice | Technology |
| Disaster Relief | International | Violence |
| Discipleship | Literacy | Other: _____ |

My top three issue passions are:

1. _____

2. _____

3. _____

# IDENTIFYING YOUR SPIRITUAL GIFTS

Read and score each of the following questions according to the following scale:

**0 = Not at all; has never occurred**

**1 = Rarely applies; seldom happens.**

**2 = Occasionally; happens once in a while.**

**3 = Frequently; occurs more often than not.**

**4 = Most of the time; consistently applies.**

Answer these questions according to who you are, not who you would like to be or think you ought to be. Put your score in the box to the immediate right of each question. Once you have completed all questions, transfer your answers to the corresponding numbered block on the table on page 192.

1. I can do many things at once. ☐

2. I would like to start churches in areas that need a strong local church. ☐

3. I can easily distinguish between right and wrong. ☐

4. I find myself sharing my Christian journey with others. ☐

5. It is easy for me to persuade others to get involved in areas of ministry. ☐

6. Trusting God to answer prayers regarding difficult situations is easy for me. ☐

7. I love to give resources to people or projects needing assistance. ☐

8. People have said that my prayers have assisted them in their healing. ☐

9. I enjoy doing smaller tasks that no one else will do. ☐

10. I can interpret when others speak in tongues. ☐

11. I receive information that I sense came from the Holy Spirit considering others. ☐

12. I feel empathy toward those who are less fortunate. ☐

13. I have been used by God to perform miracles. ☐

14. I love to guide others toward spiritual health, growth, and maturity. ☐

15. I feel compelled to share truth that has been impressed in my mind by God. ☐

16. I can find scriptural insights easily and desire to communicate these to others. ☐

17. I feel compelled to speak in tongues often. ☐

18. People often ask me for advice regarding their important decisions. ☐

19. I have the ability to work well under pressure. ☐

20. I would be willing to relocate to start a new church plant. ☐

21. I am able to distinguish between a person's real needs and possible false needs. ☐

22. I like to find new ways to develop relationships with unchurched people. ☐

23. I enjoy giving biblical advice to help people make right choices. ☐

24. I believe God to accomplish great things in my life and those around me. ☐

25. I give above and beyond my tithe to further projects or programs that fulfill God's purposes. ☐

26. I find myself praying for sick people, knowing that God can heal them. ☐

27. I would rather serve others than have others serve me. ☐

28. When people speak in tongues, I sense a stirring to interpret. ☐

29. I perceive information regarding other people without others telling me the information. ☐

30. I enjoy assisting those who are facing difficult situations. ☐

31. People say that I have been used in their lives to see a miracle take place. ☐

32. I have compassion for those in need and find myself assisting them through the process. ☐

33. I sense insights concerning the future. ☐

34. I can impart knowledge and skills in a manner that makes it easy for others to learn and apply. ☐

35. God has used me to speak in an unlearned language to a group of people. ☐

36. It is easy to identify practical solutions, where others seem confused. ☐

37. I like to take on what appear to be complex challenges. ☐

38. I find myself thinking about church-planting often. ☐

39. My first impressions of a person's motives are often true. ☐

40. I am successful at applying the Gospel to connect with a person's need or circumstance. ☐

41. I find myself directing people to God's promises by offering them hope. ☐

42. I am convinced that God's Word dictates my circumstance and circumstances don't dictate my faith. ☐

43. Charitable giving is a high priority in my life. ☐

44. I look for opportunities to pray for those who are sick. ☐

45. I prefer to function behind the scenes than in a more visible role. ☐

46. God directs me to translate the meaning of someone speaking in tongues. ☐

47. I receive impressions regarding certain people or circumstances. ☐

48. I like to practically help those who cannot help themselves. ☐

49. "Signs and wonders" occur when I am ministering to others. ☐

50. I seek to help others grow in Christ. ☐

51. The Scriptures come alive to me regarding others' lives. ☐

52. I enjoy instructing people and see positive change as a result of my instruction. ☐

53. I have been used to edify others by using tongues as the primary tool of edification. ☐

54. When talking with someone regarding a personal challenge, I sense special insight regarding their situation. ☐

55. I enjoy organizing people and programs to achieve great goals. ☐

56. Ministries that start new churches get my attention. ☐

57. I find myself able to "read between the lines." ☐

58. I openly communicate my relationship with Christ and love when others ask me about my faith. ☐

59. I am able to confront others to develop spiritual health, growth, and maturity. ☐

60. My ability to move forward in a God-given task is not hindered by a lack of support or resistance. ☐

61. I find fulfillment in seeing others blessed through giving to their needs. ☐

62. I possess a personal passion to see others healed. ☐

63. I like to take on tasks that help others to succeed. ☐

64. It is easy for me to understand what someone is saying in tongues. ☐

65. God reveals to me the source to a person's problem, illness, or need. ☐

66. I can see God's potential in every person regardless of their handicap or limitation. ☐

67. I have faith to believe that God can use me to accomplish the impossible. ☐

68. I enjoy sharing truth with others to guide them in moving to be more like Jesus. ☐

69. I am stirred in services or gatherings to communicate something that is burning in my heart. ☐

70. People have said that my instruction has helped them to better understand a concept, truth, or skill. ☐

71. After speaking in tongues, someone has interpreted my utterance. ☐

72. I seem to have a special ability to solve problems. ☐

73. I like to figure out how to accomplish certain goals and delegate them. ☐

74. I would like to oversee many churches and equip local church pastors. ☐

75. I can sense when evil forces are at work in a person or situation. ☐

76. Looking for opportunities to discuss spiritual matters with unbelievers excites me. ☐

77. I like to strengthen those who are spiritually weak. ☐

78. I trust God in any situation where the desired result cannot be guaranteed only by human efforts. ☐

79. I give my personal belongings to those in greater need, knowing God will bless me in return. ☐

80. God has used me as His vessel to heal others. ☐

81. I readily use my talents to help whenever needed, regardless of the task. ☐

82. People consider me to be a person who translates the meaning of a message delivered in tongues to a group of people. ☐

83. God gives me specific direction in assisting people in finding a solution to their problems. ☐

84. I feel compelled to offer comfort to those who are in a seemingly impossible situation. ☐

85. Extraordinary things take place when I pray for impossible situations. ☐

86. I like to help guide people through all areas of their lives in fulfilling their potential. ☐

87. I see pictures or visions for certain people concerning a situation or circumstance they are facing. ☐

88. I love to study because I realize that communicating these truths will bring change in the lives of others. ☐

89. I sense God wanting to use me to speak in tongues to believers during gatherings. ☐

90. I can identify the best course of action where many other conflicting options exist. ☐

| | | | | | | TOTAL |
|---|---|---|---|---|---|---|
| Administration/ Ruling | 1 | 19 | 37 | 55 | 73 | |
| Apostle/Pioneer | 2 | 20 | 38 | 56 | 74 | |
| Discernment | 3 | 21 | 39 | 57 | 75 | |
| Evangelism | 4 | 22 | 40 | 58 | 76 | |
| Exhortation | 5 | 23 | 41 | 59 | 77 | |
| Faith | 6 | 24 | 42 | 60 | 78 | |
| Giving | 7 | 25 | 43 | 61 | 79 | |
| Healing | 8 | 26 | 44 | 62 | 80 | |
| Helps/Serving | 9 | 27 | 45 | 63 | 81 | |
| Interpretation | 10 | 28 | 46 | 64 | 82 | |
| Knowledge | 11 | 29 | 47 | 65 | 83 | |
| Mercy | 12 | 30 | 48 | 66 | 84 | |
| Miracles | 13 | 31 | 49 | 67 | 85 | |
| Pastor/Shepherd | 14 | 32 | 50 | 68 | 86 | |
| Prophecy | 15 | 33 | 51 | 69 | 87 | |
| Teaching | 16 | 34 | 52 | 70 | 88 | |
| Tongues | 17 | 35 | 53 | 71 | 89 | |
| Wisdom | 18 | 36 | 54 | 72 | 90 | |

| SPIRITUAL GIFT | DESCRIPTION | SCRIPTURAL REFERENCES |
|---|---|---|
| Administration/ Ruling | **The gift of Administration** is the divine ability to understand and effectively perform tasks that make an organization function properly. This includes the ability to plan and organize certain goals to reach ministry objectives. | Luke 14:28-30 Acts 6:1-7 Romans 12:8 1 Corinthians 12:28 |
| Apostle/Pioneer | **The gift of Apostle/Pioneer** is the divine ability that God gives to members of the body of Christ to exercise leadership over multiple churches. | Acts 13:2-3 Romans 1:5 1 Corinthians 12:28-29 Ephesians 4:11-12 |
| Discernment | **The gift of Discernment** is the divine ability to comprehend with assurance whether a source of communication or situation is derived from a godly, human, or satanic source. | Matthew 16:21-23 Acts 5:1-11 Acts 16:16-18 1 Corinthians 12:10 1 John 4:1-6 |
| Evangelism | **The gift of Evangelism** is the divine ability to communicate the Gospel of Jesus Christ effectively to unbelievers, resulting in salvation and onward progress toward spiritual health, growth, and maturity. | Luke 19:1-10 Acts 8:26-40 Ephesians 4:11 |
| Exhortation | **The gift of Exhortation** is the divine ability to support, strengthen, uplift, and counsel those in a special way, resulting in them feeling helped and healed. | Acts 14:22 Romans 12:8 1 Timothy 4:13 Hebrews 10:25 |
| Faith | **The gift of Faith** is the divine ability to embrace with unwavering confidence God's promises and purposes and His ability to perform them. | Acts 11:22-24 Romans 4:18-21 1 Corinthians 12:9 Hebrews 11 |

| SPIRITUAL GIFT | DESCRIPTION | SCRIPTURAL REFERENCES |
|---|---|---|
| Giving | The gift of Giving is the divine ability to contribute one's finances and other resources liberally and cheerfully beyond the level expected of all believers for the benefit of the kingdom of God. | Mark 12:41-44<br>Romans 12:8<br>2 Corinthians 8:1-7<br>2 Corinthians 9:2-8 |
| Healing | The gift of Healing is the divine ability to serve as a vessel which God uses to restore people to wholeness. This would include physical, spiritual, and emotional areas of one's life. | Acts 3:1-10<br>Acts 5:12-16<br>Acts 9:32-35<br>Acts 28:7-10<br>1 Corinthians 12:9 |
| Helps/Serving | The gift of Helps/Serving is the divine ability to devote one's personal talents and abilities toward the lives and ministry of others. | Acts 6:1-4<br>Acts 9:36<br>Romans 12:7<br>Romans 16:1-2<br>1 Corinthians 12:28 |
| Interpretation | The gift of Interpretation is the divine ability to translate a message to a known language from an unknown tongue spoken to a body of believers in tongues. | 1 Corinthians 12:10, 30<br>1 Corinthians 14:5, 13, 26-28 |
| Knowledge | The gift of the word of Knowledge is the divine ability to know facts that could not otherwise be known. | Mark 2:6-8<br>Acts 5:1-11<br>1 Corinthians 12:8<br>2 Corinthians 11:6 |
| Mercy | The gift of Mercy is the divine ability to see others in need and be moved with empathy and compassion, resulting in meaningful actions that help better the distressing circumstances of the person being ministered to. | Matthew 20:29-34<br>Luke 10:25-37<br>Acts 11:28-30<br>Romans 12:8 |
| Miracles | The gift of Miracles is the divine ability to be used by the Holy Spirit in a supernatural way to perform powerful acts that alter the course of nature and result in glorifying God. | John 2:1-11<br>Acts 20:7-12<br>Romans 15:18-19<br>1 Corinthians 12:10, 28 |

| SPIRITUAL GIFT | DESCRIPTION | SCRIPTURAL REFERENCES |
|---|---|---|
| Pastor/Shepherd | **The gift of Pastor/Shepherd** is the divine ability to assume a personal responsibility to care for and lead others into receiving greater depths of spiritual health, growth, and maturity. | John 10:1-18<br>Ephesians 4:11-12<br>1 Timothy 3:1-7<br>1 Peter 5:1-3 |
| Prophecy | **The gift of Prophecy** is the divine ability to receive, interpret, and deliver a message from God in a timely manner for edification, repentance, understanding, and/or correction. | Acts 15:32<br>Romans 12:6<br>1 Corinthians 12:28<br>Ephesians 4:11-14<br>2 Peter 1:19-20 |
| Teaching | **The gift of Teaching** is the divine ability to receive God-given truths from God's Word and communicate them in a relevant way, resulting in others learning and applying those truths in their personal walk with Christ. | Acts 18:24-28<br>Acts 20:20-21<br>1 Corinthians 12:28<br>Ephesians 4:11-13 |
| Tongues | **The gift of Tongues** is the divine ability to receive and communicate a message delivered by God to His people through a heavenly inspired language, different than speaking to God in an unknown language during private devotion and edification. | Mark 16:17<br>Acts 2:1-13<br>Acts 10:44-46<br>1 Corinthians 12:10, 28-30<br>1 Corinthians 14:1-33 |
| Wisdom | **The gift of the word of Wisdom** is the divine ability to know the mind of God toward a certain situation in a manner that gives you supernatural understanding, resulting in others receiving God-given direction and clarity to make proper decisions. | Acts 6:3<br>1 Corinthians 2:1-13<br>1 Corinthians 12:8<br>James 3:13-18<br>2 Peter 3:15 |

# CLARIFYING YOUR TALENTS AND ABILITIES

Please take a moment to read through the list of talents and abilities, checking off every item where you perceive yourself to have a special ability or talent. If there is an area that is not listed, please add it. Once you have completed checking off all appropriate boxes, answer the questions that follow.

**PROFESSIONAL SERVICES**

☐ Mental Health
☐ Counseling
☐ Social Work
☐ Accounting
☐ Bookkeeping
☐ Medical
☐ Nursing
☐ Paramedic
☐ Legal
☐ Law Enforcement
☐ Landscaping
☐ Unemployment
☐ Daycare
☐ Public Relations
☐ Advertising
☐ Computer Programming
☐ Journalism/Writing

**CONSTRUCTION**

☐ General Contractor
☐ Drywall
☐ Carpenter
☐ Cabinets
☐ Electrician
☐ Plumbing
☐ Heating/AC
☐ Painting
☐ Masonry
☐ Roofing

**MISSIONS**

☐ Missionary
☐ Evangelism

**ART**

☐ Painting
☐ Layout
☐ Graphics

☐ Screen Printing
☐ Photography
☐ Decorating
☐ Crafts
☐ Interior Design

**MECHANICAL**

☐ Copier Repair
☐ Auto Mechanic
☐ Small Engine Repair
☐ Mower Repair
☐ Machinist

**THEATRICAL**

☐ Acting
☐ Dancing
☐ Puppets
☐ Audio Production
☐ Sound/Mixing
☐ Lighting

☐ Set Design
☐ Set Construction
☐ Stage Hand
☐ Script Writer

**WORKING WITH**

☐ Handicapped
☐ Hearing Impaired
☐ Incarcerated
☐ Learning Disabilities
☐ Shut-ins
☐ Housing for Homeless
☐ Hospital Visitation

**TEACHING/
ASSISTING**

☐ Preschool
☐ Elementary
☐ Junior High

☐ Senior High
☐ Singles
☐ Couples
☐ Men's Groups
☐ Women's Groups
☐ Tutoring

**OFFICE SKILLS**

☐ Typing
☐ Word Processing
☐ Receptionist
☐ Office Manager
☐ Data Entry
☐ Filing/Photocopying
☐ Transcription

**GENERAL HELPS**

☐ Catering/Cooking
☐ Cashier

☐ Childcare
☐ Food Service
☐ Gardening
☐ Grounds Maintenance
☐ Transportation
☐ Telephoning
☐ Mailing
☐ Sports Instructor

**MUSICAL**

☐ Singer
☐ Composer
☐ Instrument_____

**OTHER**

☐ _____
☐ _____
☐ _____

## Summarizing Your Talents and Abilities

What talents and/or abilities do you feel best about?

_____
_____
_____
_____
_____

What most interests you?

_____
_____
_____
_____
_____

What are some of your hobbies?

_____

_____

_____

_____

_____

What are your greatest talents?

_____

_____

_____

_____

_____

How do you think you could use the abilities you checked to serve in your church?

_____

_____

_____

_____

_____

# LEARNING ABOUT YOUR PERSONAL MAKEUP

Please take a moment to review the following chart. For each item, select the trait that best describes you—number 1 being most like the trait on the left hand side, the number 5 being most like the trait on the right hand side. Select the behavior that reflects who you naturally are, not what would be expected of you by someone else.

Add up the total of each section and enter the sum total in the appropriate boxes (X and Y). Turn to the following page and complete the process.

## How Do I Handle Things?

| | | | |
|---|---|---|---|
| **I lean toward** | Evaluating the options | 1 2 3 4 5 | Making prompt decisions |
| **I enjoy** | Trying new things | 1 2 3 4 5 | A set agenda |
| **When I wake up, I like to** | Allow my day to unfold | 1 2 3 4 5 | Plan my day |
| **During my free time I tend to** | Be spontaneous | 1 2 3 4 5 | Have a plan |
| **When plans change, I typically** | Go with the flow | 1 2 3 4 5 | Get frustrated |
| **Maintaining a budget** | Is difficult | 1 2 3 4 5 | Is enjoyable |

How do I handle things?   X = [ ]

## How Am I Motivated?

| | | | |
|---|---|---|---|
| **When asked to get involved, I am more interested in** | What I need to do | 1 2 3 4 5 | Who else will be involved |
| **I like to** | Do | 1 2 3 4 5 | Talk |
| **I would rather** | Complete something | 1 2 3 4 5 | Help someone |

| I enjoy | Working with people | 1 2 3 4 5 | Working with things |
|---|---|---|---|
| I am motivated by | Meeting a goal or deadline | 1 2 3 4 5 | Building relationships |
| During my free time I prefer to | Work on projects | 1 2 3 4 5 | Hang out with people |

How am I motivated?   Y = [          ]

On this scale, mark your X and Y axis using the numbers in the boxes from the two previous sections. Draw a horizontal line through the X-axis where your score is recorded, and a vertical line through the Y-axis where your score is recorded. You can identify your personal makeup by the intersection of the two lines. See example to the right.

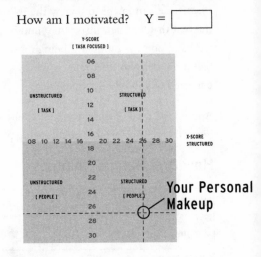

**Your Personal Makeup**

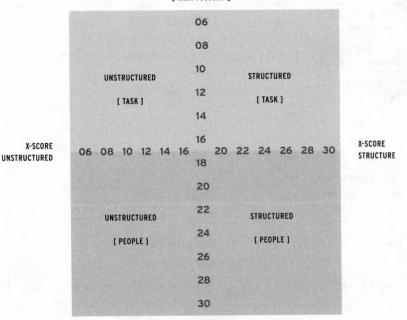

# MAKING SENSE OF YOUR LIFE EXPERIENCES

Take a moment to think about how your life experiences (ministry, family and life, education, career, challenges, health, financial) have helped shape you for serving opportunities. Write your thoughts below:

**Ministry**
What past ministry experiences have you had?

_____

_____

_____

_____

_____

How have these experiences helped you?

_____

_____

_____

_____

How could you use these ministry experiences to serve others?

_____

_____

_____

_____

**Family and Life**
What areas of your family and life experiences stick out most to you (i.e., where you lived, how you were raised, religious background)?

Do you see any connection between these family/life experiences and how you could use these to serve? If so, how?

_____

_____

_____

_____

_____


### Education

What type of special education have you experienced that could be used to serve others (i.e., computer, administration, video, layout and graphic design, counseling, auto mechanics, carpentry)?

_____

_____

_____

_____

_____


### Career

How do you think you could use what you have learned in your career experiences to serve others?

_____

_____

_____

_____

_____


### Challenges

What is the most painful experience that has happened in your life (i.e., divorce, addiction, past sin, disease, death of a loved one)?

_____

_____

_____

_____

_____

What have you learned from that experience?

_____
_____
_____
_____
_____

How do you think that experience could be used to help others?

_____
_____
_____
_____
_____

## Health

Are there any specific health issues in your life that would be worth mentioning?

_____
_____
_____
_____
_____

Paired with your life experiences, how could these health issues be used to help others facing the same challenge?

_____
_____
_____
_____
_____

### Financial

How would you describe your financial history?

_____

_____

_____

_____

_____

What financial successes and failures have you experienced?

_____

_____

_____

_____

_____

How could your financial experiences be used to help others?

_____

_____

_____

_____

_____

# DISCERNING YOUR SPIRITUAL MATURITY

Read the following statements below and evaluate yourself on a scale of 1 to 6. Write the number in the total column. Add your score and put the total in the box below. Review your results using the legend below.

| Christian Foundation Stones<br>[ 1=no ] [ 6 = yes ] | SCORE |
|---|---|
| I am a born-again believer. | |
| I have been water baptized after my conversion. | |
| I have been baptized in the Holy Spirit. | |
| I belong to a local church. | |

| Spiritual Disciplines<br>[ 1=never, 2=rarely, 3=sometimes, 4=often, 5=usually, 6=always ] | SCORE |
|---|---|
| I read my Bible daily. | |
| I have a quality time of prayer daily. | |
| I attend church services weekly. | |
| I serve in an area ministry. | |
| I belong to a small group. | |
| I am faithful in giving tithes and offerings. | |
| I share my faith with the unchurched and spiritual seekers. | |
| I am helping others in their journey toward spiritual maturity. | |

| Christian Character<br>[ 1=never, 2=rarely, 3=sometimes, 4=often, 5=usually, 6=always ] | SCORE |
|---|---|
| I apply God's Word to every situation. | |
| I find myself praying more than complaining. | |
| I find it easy to serve others. | |
| I enjoy helping those in need. | |
| I seek to live in a manner that is exemplary to those around me. | |
| I am submissive and loyal to authority figures in my life. | |
| I generally have a great attitude about life's circumstances. | |
| I am not easily offended. | |
| I am always a part of the solution, not the problem. | |
| I like to give more than receive. | |
| My finances are in order. | |
| I abstain from damaging addictions. | |
| I am constantly working to change bad habits. | |
| I carefully guard my thought life and take practical steps to keep it pure. | |
| My priorities are in order. | |
| I perceive myself to be a humble person. | |
| **TOTAL** | |

## Score Results

| | |
|---|---|
| **160+** | Congratulations! You should be teaching others. |
| **125–160** | Great job! You're living life on purpose. |
| **100–125** | You're doing a fine job. Keep up the great work! |
| **75–100** | You're well on your way, but don't stop now … |
| **50–75** | You're heading in the right direction. Give yourself an extra boost. |
| **28–50** | The good news is you have room for growth. Give it all you've got! |

What areas did you score 3 or less in?

_____

_____

_____

_____

What changes will you make to improve in these areas?

_____

_____

_____

_____

# MAKING PRIORITY ADJUSTMENTS

Please take a few minutes to determine the time spent each week doing each of the following items. Write your answers in the Current Hours Per Week column. It's very important that you fill in the amount of hours you spend in each area based on *real time*. Some areas may be hard to measure, but give it your best guess. This is only a tool for you to see where your time is going.

The second column is designed to challenge you to reconsider what adjustments are most necessary, and where you might reallocate your time. Prayerfully consider what adjustments you'd like to make in each of these areas to better align your priorities with your purpose. Indicate your new goals in the column on the right. Remember, there are only 168 hours in a week. See how you spend them now.

| Priority Item | Current Hrs./Week | New Goal Hrs./Week |
|---|---|---|
| Time spent in personal devotions | | |
| Time spent in church services | | |
| Time devoted toward purpose, ministry | | |
| Time spent serving others | | |
| Time spent with spouse | | |
| Time spent with children | | |
| Time spent with family and friends | | |
| Time spent reaching the unchurched and spiritual seekers | | |
| Time spent mentoring and/or discipling others | | |
| Time spent working (career, housewife, etc.) | | |

| | | |
|---|---|---|
| Time spent in financial matters (budgeting, investing) | | |
| Time spent toward increasing physical fitness | | |
| Time spent invested in personal growth (books, CDs, etc.) | | |
| Time spent in entertainment | | |
| Time spent in hobbies | | |
| Time spent watching TV/videos, on the Internet | | |
| Time spent sleeping | | |
| Other: | | |
| **TOTAL WEEKLY HOURS (168 hours in week)** | | |

# REVIEWING YOUR SCHEDULE

Use the following table to identify the number of hours you may be available to serve. Insert the number of hours you can serve in any of the available boxes. Checking a block of time does not mean you will serve during all of those times; it simply helps you to see *when* you're available. This will allow you to match your availability with the serving opportunities in your local church.

After you've filled out the times you are available, take a few minutes to answer the remaining questions. They will help you and a ministry leader at your church make the best decision regarding your serving opportunities.

• **Flexible**—Availability includes:

|           | Monday | Tuesday | Wednesday | Thursday | Friday | Saturday | Sunday |
|-----------|--------|---------|-----------|----------|--------|----------|--------|
| Morning   |        |         |           |          |        |          |        |
| Afternoon |        |         |           |          |        |          |        |
| Evening   |        |         |           |          |        |          |        |

• **1-3** hours per week

• **3-5** hours per week

• **5-10** hours per week

• **10+** hours per week

• **Not Sure**

• **Seasonal** (i.e., Christmas programs, during the school year)

• **Occasional** (i.e., special events, conferences, hospitality, camps, retreats)

• **As Needed** (i.e., grief support, meals)

Do you foresee any significant changes in your life in the near future (i.e. moving to another city, changing churches, pregnancy, job promotion or change)?

_____

_____

_____

_____

_____

List any seasons where your schedule, work, or family may limit your availability.

_____

_____

_____

_____

_____

Please list any other ministry positions where you are currently serving, along with the day and time you serve.

_____

_____

_____

_____

_____

# ENDNOTES

## Chapter Zero: Confessions of a Squandered Paper Clip

1. *http://www.travelfinders.com/html/business.html*, Sound Bytes. Accessed June 24, 2005.

---

## Chapter 1: On a Journey ... Going Somewhere

1. *http://www.markbarry.com*, "The Official Site of 'The Lawn Chair Pilot'" (see entire story, associated articles, photos, and audio files of actual flight), accessed June 24, 2005; *The New York Times*. December 19, 1982.

2. Myrna Oliver, "Larry Walters: Soared to Fame on Lawn Chair," *The Los Angeles Times*, November 24, 1993.

3. "Ogling Google: 'Jesus' *is* bigger than 'The Beatles,'" *http://www.pressflex.com/news/fullstory.php/aid/42/Ogling_Google:__Jesus__is_bigger_than__The_Beatles_.htm*, accessed April 17, 2006.

4. Paul Lee Tan, *Encyclopedia of 7700 Illustrations* (Rockville, MD: Assurance Publishers, 1979), 1471.

---

## Chapter 2: Lucky You

1. Personal interview with Kevin Conner, January 19, 2006. Excerpts taken from an interview in the "Evangel NOW!," written by Paul Gallagher. Other comments were taken from an interview conducted at City Bible Church with the Generation Church staff.

2. *http://www.barna.org/flexpage.aspx?page=topic&topicid=5*, accessed April 17, 2006.

3. Ryan Pearson, "Stolen 320-Year-Old Cello Is Found," *Duluth Superior Tribune*, May 19, 2004.

---

## Chapter 3: Surprise! You've Got a Purpose

1. *http://www.metroministries.com/bill.asp?ID=9*, accessed April 15, 2006.

2. Tommy Barnett and Lela Gilbert, *Dream Again* (Lake Mary, FL, Creation House, 1998), 76–80.

3. Kevin Conner, *The Foundations of Christian Doctrine* (Portland, OR: City Christian Publishing, 1980), 129.

4. Daniel Roth, "Seeing the World on Ten Coffees a Day," *FORTUNE*, July 12, 2004.

5. Michael Hodgin, *1001 More Humorous Illustrations for Public Speaking* (Grand Rapids, MI: Zondervan, 1998), 268.

6. Cynthia Kersey, *Unstoppable* (Naperville, IL: Sourcebooks, Inc., 1998), 47.

## Chapter 4: Unfathomable You

1. Phone interview with Stephanie Fast, July 2005.

2. *http://astronomy.swin.edu.au/~gmackie/billions.html*, accessed May 10, 2006.

3. Dr. Jon McNeff, "Closer than a brother," *http://www.northcreek.org/resources/sermons/notes/2005/082105_CloserThanA.pdf*.

4. From Barnes' Notes, Electronic Database. © 1997 by Biblesoft.

## Chapter 5: Living the Dream

1. *http://www.cleanwaterforhaiti.org/cleanwaterfactsheet.pdf*, accessed May 22, 2006.

2. Personal interview with Craig Fasler, May 22, 2006.

3. *http://www.brainyquote.com/quotes/quotes/r/ralphwaldo108797.html*, accessed July 13, 2006.

4. There are two passion expressions listed that some might interpret as spiritual gifts: hospitality and intercession. I do not claim or desire to be the authoritative word on this subject, but through much study and godly counsel, I have concluded that these two areas can not only be spiritual gifts but also passions.

5. Bruce Bugbee, *What You Do Best in the Body of Christ* (Grand Rapids, MI: Zondervan, 1995), 30–31.

6. *http://www.brainyquote.com/quotes/quotes/s/samuelbutl149756.html*, accessed April 17, 2006.

7. Kersey, 82.

8. Ibid., 297.

9. Marcus Buckingham and Donald O. Clifton, PhD, *Now, Discover Your Strengths* (New York: The Free Press, 2001), 21.

## Chapter 6: How'd I Do That? And Why?

1. Personal interview with Ed Schefter, August 23, 2005.

2. "Awareness of Spiritual Gifts Is Changing," February 5, 2001, *http://www.barna.org/FlexPage.aspx?Page=BarnaUpdate&BarnaUpdateID=81*.

3. This story has been told by the author for many years ... But it is very possible that it is merely an urban legend.

4. Raymond McHenry, *McHenry's Quips, Quotes & Other Notes* (Peabody, MA: Hendrickson Publishers, 1998), 231.

5. "Amy Dodson Reigns Supreme for Challenged Females," *www.michiganrunner.net/news/amy_dodson0905.html*, accessed August 13, 2005.

6. Gary Beasley, Francis Anfuso, Marc Estes, Tom Stamman, *Complete Evangelism* (Lake Tahoe, CA: Christian Equippers International, 1991), 427–442.

## Chapter 7: Second Nature

1. *http://www.habitat.org/how/millard.aspx*, accessed August 22, 2005. *http://www.habitat.org/how/historytext.aspx*, accessed July 13, 2006. Excerpts also taken from Cynthia Kersey, *Unstoppable* (Naperville, IL, Sourcebooks, 1998), 22–25.

2. Buckingham and Clifton, 50–51.

3. George Brunstad, "It wasn't all bad," *THE WEEK*, September 10, 2004, 4.

4. Buckingham and Clifton, 48.

5. "Using Your Talents," *http://www.publiceye.org/ifas/fw/9609/guide.html*, accessed August 24, 2005.

## Chapter 8: Mirror, Mirror on the Wall ...

1. Phone interview with Linda Bremner, August 2005. Additional information found on *http://www.lovelettersinc.org*.

2. Taken from NetWork Participant's Guide by Don Cousins, Bill Hybels, Bruce Bugbee. Copyright ©1994 by Willow Creek Community Church. Used by permission of the Zondervan Corporation.

3. Rick Warren, *The Purpose Driven Life* (Grand Rapids, MI: Zondervan, 2002), 246.

## Chapter 9: Hurts So Good

1. Phone interview with Zarah Dupree, September 2005.

2. *http://en.thinkexist.com/quotes/charles_r._swindoll*, accessed April 17, 2006.

3. *www.truettcathy.com*, accessed September 28, 2005.

## Chapter 10: It's Time to Grow Up

1. Personal interview with Dick Iverson, September 2005.

2. *http://en.thinkexist.com/quotes/william_booth*, accessed May 10, 2006.

3. "Americans Identify What They Want Out of Life," April 26, 2000, *http://www.barna.org/FlexPage.aspx?Page=BarnaUpdate&BarnaUpdateID=57*, accessed September 13, 2005.

4. *The Baptist Standard*, May 12, 1993, 24; *Facts & Trends*, May 1988, 3.

5. Frank Damazio, *Vision Management* (Portland, OR: City Christian Publishing, 2002).

## Chapter 11: Spinning Plates

1. Phone interview with Mike White, September 2005.

2. Robert J. Morgan, *Nelson's Complete Book of Stories, Illustrations and Quotes* (Nashville, TN: Thomas Nelson Publishers, Inc., 2001), 513.

3. Bob Buford, *Halftime* (Grand Rapids, MI: Zondervan, 1994), 23.

4. McHenry, 48.

5. Buford, 82.

6. McHenry, 121.

7. Ted Engstrom, *What in the World Is God Doing* (Word Books).

## Chapter 12: Here Comes the Bride

1. Personal interview with Jeanette Moore, December 14, 2004.

2. Kevin Conner, *The Church in the New Testament* (Portland, OR: City Christian Publishing, 1982), 24.

3. Bill Scheidler, *Principles of Church Life* (Portland, OR: City Christian Publishing, 1976), 78.

4. The World Factbook, "Rank Order-Population," *http://www.cia.gov/cia/publications/factbook/rankorder/2119rank.html*, accessed April 17, 2006.

5. "The State of the Church, 2000," March 21, 2000, *http://www.barna.org/FlexPage.aspx?Page=BarnaUpdate&BarnaUpdateID=49*, accessed September 18, 2005.

6. "Number of Unchurched Adults Has Nearly Doubled Since 1991," *http://www.barna.org/FlexPage.aspx?Page=BarnaUpdate&BarnaUpdateID=163*, accessed September 21, 2005.

7. Francis Anfuso and Gary Beasley, *Complete Evangelism* (Lake Tahoe, CA: Christian Equippers International, 1991), 23.

8. Dave Ramsey, *The Total Money Makeover* (Nashville, TN: Thomas Nelson, Inc., 2003), 11, 19.

9. Morgan, 123.

10. *http://www.barna.org/flexpage.aspx?page=resource&resourceid=15*, accessed May 10, 2006.

11. Joshua Harris, *Stop Dating the Church* (Sisters, OR: Multnomah Publishers, Inc., 2004), 30.

12. Warren, 132.

13. Morgan, 129.

## Chapter 13: Finding Your Place on the Team
1. Personal interview with Joseph Branchflower, September 2005.

## Chapter 14: Giving It All You've Got
1. "Chinese Christians Face Persecution," *The Commission*, June 2002, 26.

2. Robertson's Word Pictures in the New Testament, Electronic Database. © 1997 by Biblesoft. Robertson's Word Pictures in the New Testament. © 1985 by Broadman Press.

3. Ted Haggard, *Foolish No More* (Colorado Springs, CO: Waterbrook Press, 2005), 38.

4. Ibid., 35–36.

5. *http://www.bible.org/illus.asp?topic_id=317*, accessed May 10, 2006.

## Chapter 15: The Day After
1. "Strength for Living," April 30, 2004, *http://www.ontrack.org/Content/RadioSpotlight.asp?RadioSpotlightid=2888*, accessed August 12, 2005.

2. A Farewell Tribute, *A Life Lived Well* (a commemorative publication produced by Worldwide Challenge Magazine in partnership with Journey Group, Inc.)

3. Ibid.

4. "America Needs to Pray for Revival, Bill Bright Tells Southern Baptists" *http://www.goodnewsetc.com/082EVNG3.htm*, accessed April 17, 2006.

5. "Strength for Living."

6. *http://www.ontrack.org/documents/2891.htm*, accessed April 20, 2006.

7. A Farewell Tribute, *A Life Lived Well*, 11.

8. Frank Bartleman, *Azusa Street* (South Plainfield, NJ: Bridge Publishing, 1980), 58.

9. Robert E. Coleman, *The Master Plan of Evangelism*, *http://www.navigators.org/resources/shared/ministries/prison/10Multiply.pdf*, accessed April 17, 2006.

10. Personal interview with Donna Lasit, October 17, 2005.

11. *http://www.catholicculture.org/docs/doc_view.cfm?recnum=185*, accessed April 17, 2006. *http://nobelprize.org/peace/laureates/1979/teresa-bio.html*, accessed April 17, 2006. *http://www.vatican.va/news_services/liturgy/saints/ns_lit_doc_20031019_madre-teresa_en.html*, accessed April 17, 2006.

# ADDITIONAL RESOURCES

For additional resources or
to contact the author directly,
please visit

*www.marcestes.com*

where you'll find information about
other books by the author,
small group resources,
and a study guide for *What Now.*

# [RELEVANTBOOKS]

## FOR MORE INFORMATION
## ABOUT OTHER RELEVANT BOOKS,

check out www.relevantbooks.com.